RAND McNALLY

DISCOVERY ATLAS OF THE UNITED STATES

Rand McNally for Kids™

Books•Maps•Atlases

Discovery Atlas of the United States

General manager: Russell L. Voisin
Executive editor: Jon M. Leverenz
Editor: Elizabeth Fagan Adelman
Production editor: Laura C. Schmidt
Manufacturing planner: Marianne Abraham

Discovery Atlas of the United States
Copyright © 1993 by Rand McNally & Company
Published and printed in the United States of
America

Portions of this book were originally
published in Rand McNally *Children's Atlas
of the United States*, copyright ©1990 by
Rand McNally. Every effort has been made to
trace the copyright holders of the photographs
in this publication. Rand McNally apologizes in
advance for any unintentional omissions and
would be pleased to insert the appropriate
acknowledgment in any subsequent edition
of this book.

Populations are 1990 census figures. City
figures do not include surrounding suburbs.

Library of Congress Cataloging-in-
Publication Data

Rand McNally and Company.
        Discovery atlas of the United States.
            p.   cm.
        At head of title: Rand McNally.
        Includes index.
        Summary: Includes maps for the fifty
states and the District of Columbia, with
illustrations of the official flags, trees, birds,
and flowers and information on important
facts and features for each jurisdiction.
            ISBN 0-528-83578-5
            1. United States--Maps for children.
[1. United States--Maps. 2. Atlases.]
I. Title.   II. Title: Rand McNally discovery
atlas of the United States
G1200.R3225   1993 <G&M>
912.73--dc20
                                                   93-18713
                                                        CIP
                                                   MAP AC

Contents

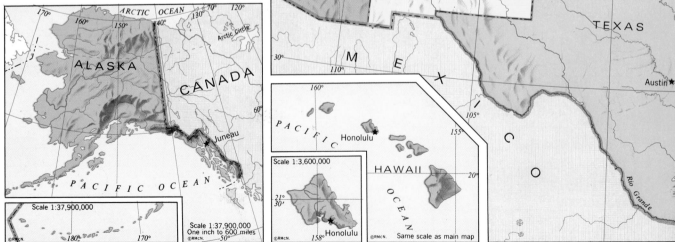

125°   130°

45°

120°

115°

110°

105°

100°

Seattle
WASHINGTON
Olympia
Portland
Salem ★
OREGON

R
O
C
K
Y

MONTANA
Helena ★

C
A

A

NORTH DAKOT
Bismarck ★

C
A

40°

C
A
S
C
A
D
E

IDAHO
Boise ★

WYOMING

M
O
U

Pierre ★
SOUTH DAKOT

35°

P
A
C
I
F
I
C

O
C
E
A
N

Sacramento ★
San Francisco

C
A
L
I
F
O
R
N
I
A

Carson City ★
NEVADA

Great
Salt Lake
Salt Lake City ★

UTAH

N
T
A
I
N
S

Cheyenne ★

Denver ★
COLORADO

NEBRASKA

KANSA

S
I
E
R
R
A

N
E
V
A
D
A

Los Angeles

San Diego

ARIZONA
Phoenix ★

Santa Fe ★

NEW MEXICO

OKLA
Oklahoma Cit

D-520500-26
COPYRIGHT BY
RAND MCNALLY & COMPANY
MADE IN U.S.A.

120°

115°

TEXAS

ARCTIC   OCEAN
170°   160°   150°   140°   130°   70°   120°
Arctic Circle

ALASKA
CANADA

Juneau ★

PACIFIC   OCEAN

Scale 1:37,900,000

180°   170°

30°
110°

160°

PACIFIC

Honolulu ★

Scale 1:3,600,000

HAWAII

21°
30'

O
C
E
A
N

158° Honolulu

Scale 1:37,900,000
One inch to 600 miles
50°

M
E
X

155°

20°

I
C
O

Austin ★

Rio Grande

Same scale as main map

100°

This map shows the United States and its major geographical features, state
capitals, and other metropolitan centers. The area of the United States is
3,539,341 square miles (9,166,851 sq. km.) and its population is 248,709,873.

Scale 1:12,600,000; one inch to 200 miles   Polyconic Proj

National capital ⊗

State capital ★   Urban area

PACIFIC TIME ZONE
MOUNTAIN TIME ZONE
BRITISH COLUMBIA
ALBERTA
SASKATCHEWAN
CANADA
UNITED STATES
PACIFIC OCEAN
WASHINGTON
OREGON
IDAHO
MONTANA
NORTH DAKOTA
SOUTH DAKOTA
WYOMING
NEBRASKA
NEVADA
UTAH
COLORADO
KANSAS
CALIFORNIA
ARIZONA
NEW MEXICO
OKLAHOMA
TEXAS
MEXICO
VANCOUVER
Victoria
Calgary
Regina
SEATTLE
TACOMA
SPOKANE
PORTLAND
Salem
Eugene
Boise
Great Falls
Helena
Billings
Bismarck
Rapid City
Cheyenne
Salt Lake City
Reno
Carson City
Sacramento
San Francisco
Oakland
San Jose
Fresno
Los Angeles
San Diego
Las Vegas
Phoenix
Tucson
Albuquerque
Santa Fe
Denver
El Paso
Ciudad Juárez
Mexicali
Monterrey
Gulf of California
ALASKA
Fairbanks
Anchorage
Juneau
RUSSIA
YUKON
NORTHWEST TERRITORIES
Arctic Ocean
Bering Sea
Gulf of Alaska
Pacific Ocean
ALEUTIAN ISLANDS
HAWAII
HAWAII-ALEUTIAN TIME ZONE
Kauai
Oahu
Molokai
Maui
Hawaii
Honolulu
© RMcN

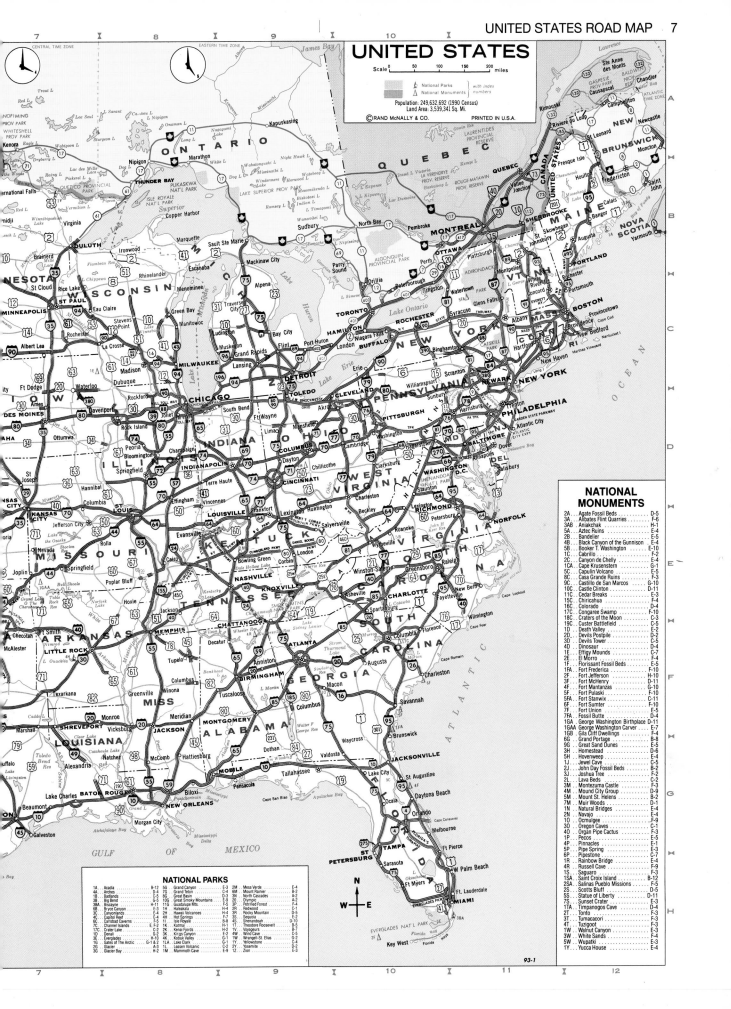

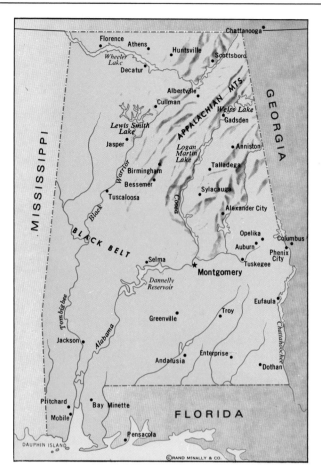

ALABAMA

Capital
Montgomery (187,106 people)

Area
50,766 square miles (131,483 sq. km.)
Rank: 28th

Population
4,062,608 people Rank: 22nd

Statehood
Dec. 14, 1819 (22nd state admitted)

Principal rivers
Alabama River, Tombigbee River

Highest point
Cheaha Mountain; 2,405 feet (733 m.)

Largest city
Birmingham (265,968 people)

Motto
We dare defend our rights

Song
"Alabama"

Famous people
George Washington Carver, Helen Keller

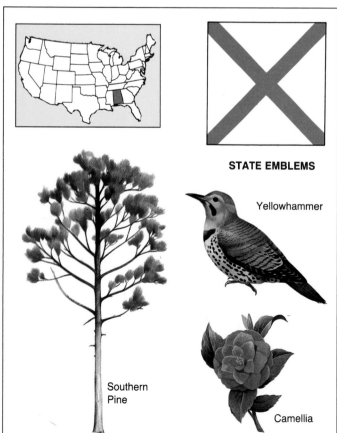

STATE EMBLEMS

Yellowhammer

Southern Pine

Camellia

Many types of spacecraft are on display at the Alabama Space and Rocket Center, near Huntsville.

© RAND MC NALLY & CO.

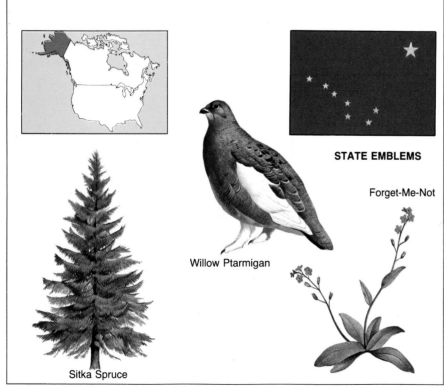

STATE EMBLEMS

Willow Ptarmigan

Forget-Me-Not

Sitka Spruce

ALASKA

Capital
Juneau (26,751 people)

Area
570,833 square miles
(1,478,451 sq. km.)
Rank: 1st

Population
551,947 people Rank: 49th

Statehood
Jan. 3, 1959 (49th state admitted)

Principal river
Yukon River

Highest point
Mount McKinley; 20,320 feet (6,194 m.)

Largest city
Anchorage (226,338 people)

Motto
North to the future

Song
"Alaska's Flag"

Famous people
Vitus Bering, Carl Eielson, Joe Juneau, William H. Seward

Phoenix has become the largest city in the Southwest.

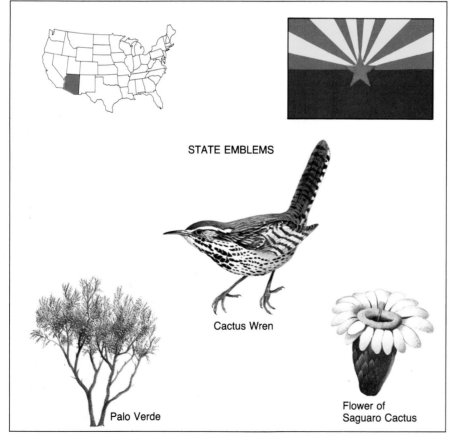

STATE EMBLEMS

Cactus Wren

Palo Verde

Flower of
Saguaro Cactus

ARIZONA

Capital and largest city
Phoenix (983,403 people)

Area
113,510 square miles
(293,990 sq. km.)
Rank: 6th

Population
3,677,985 people
Rank: 24th

Statehood
Feb. 14, 1912
(48th state admitted)

Principal rivers
Colorado River, Gila River

Highest point
Humphreys Peak; 12,633
feet (3,851 m.)

Motto
Ditat Deus (God enriches)

Song
"Arizona"

Famous people
Cochise, Geronimo, Barry
Goldwater, Zane Grey, Helen
Jacobs, Sandra Day O'Connor

ARKANSAS

Capital and largest city
Little Rock
(175,795 people)

Area
52,082 square miles
(134,892 sq. km.)
Rank: 27th

Population
2,362,239 people
Rank: 33rd

Statehood
June 15, 1836
(25th state admitted)

Principal rivers
Arkansas River,
Mississippi River,
White River

Highest point
Magazine Mountain;
2,753 feet (839 m.)

Motto
Regnat populus (The
people rule)

Song
"Arkansas"

Famous people
Hattie Caraway,
Johnny Cash, James
W. Fulbright,
Douglas MacArthur,
James S. McDonnel

STATE EMBLEMS

Mockingbird

Pine

Apple Blossom

A 216-foot (65-meter) tower at Hot Springs.

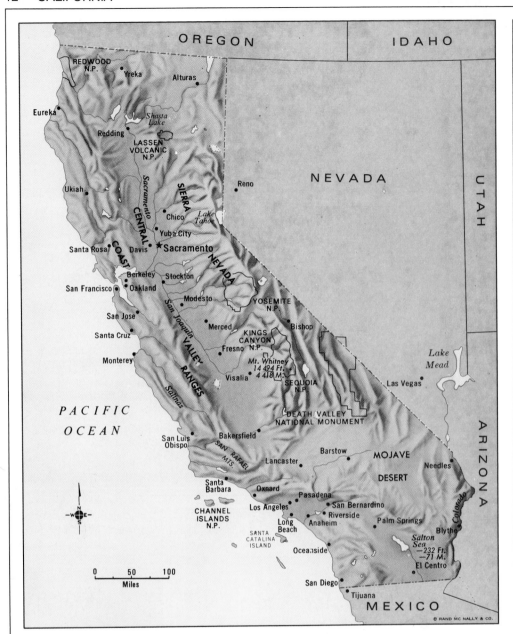

CALIFORNIA

Capital
Sacramento (369,365 people)

Area
156,297 square miles (404,807 sq. km.)
Rank: 3rd

Population
29,839,250 people
Rank: 1st

Statehood
Sept. 9, 1850 (31st state admitted)

Principal rivers
Colorado River, Sacramento River, San Joaquin River

Highest point
Mount Whitney; 14,494 feet (4,418 m.)

Largest city
Los Angeles (3,485,398 people)

Motto
Eureka (I have found it)

Song
"I Love You, California"

Famous people
Shirley Temple Black, Cesar Chavez, William Randolph Hearst, Marilyn Monroe, Ronald Reagan, Sally Ride, John Steinbeck, Earl Warren

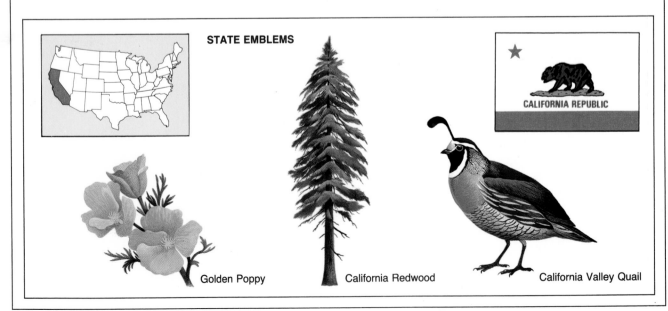

STATE EMBLEMS

Golden Poppy

California Redwood

California Valley Quail

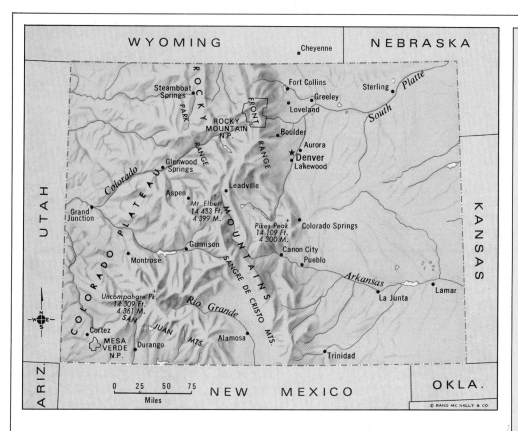

COLORADO

Capital and largest city
Denver (467,610 people)

Area
103,598 square miles (268,318 sq. km.)
Rank: 8th

Population
3,307,912 people
Rank: 26th

Statehood
Aug. 1, 1876
(38th state admitted)

Principal rivers
Arkansas River, Colorado River, South Platte River

Highest point
Mount Elbert; 14,433 feet (4,399 m.)

Motto
Nil sine numine
(Nothing without providence)

Song
"Where the Columbines Grow"

Famous people
Frederick Bonfils, M. Scott Carpenter, Douglas Fairbanks, Florence Rena Sabin, Lowell Thomas, Paul Whiteman

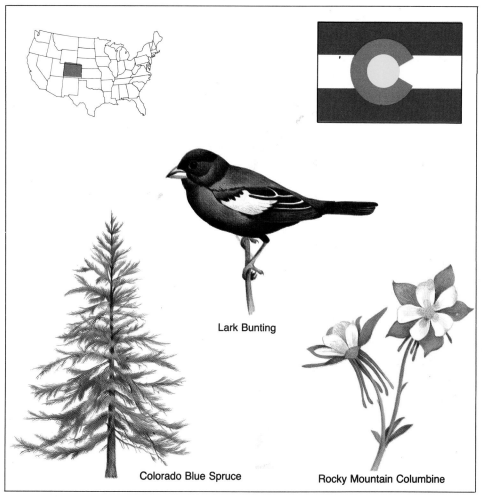

Lark Bunting

Colorado Blue Spruce

Rocky Mountain Columbine

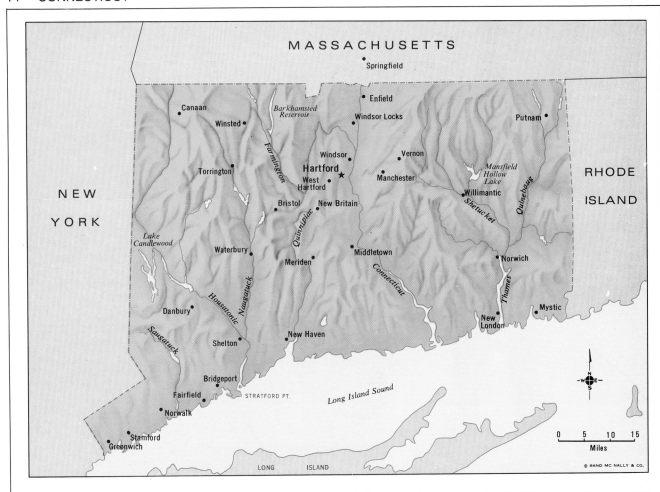

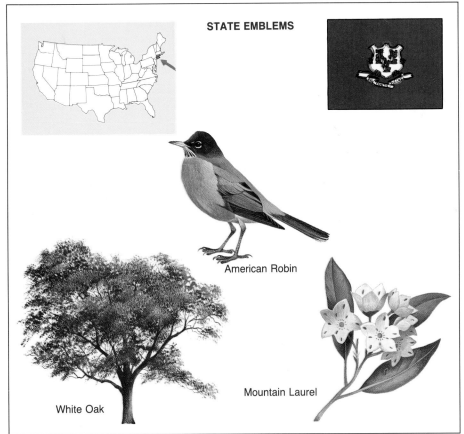

STATE EMBLEMS

American Robin

White Oak

Mountain Laurel

CONNECTICUT

Capital
Hartford (139,739 people)

Area
4,872 square miles
(12,618 sq. km.)
Rank: 48th

Population
3,295,669 people
Rank: 27th

Statehood
Jan. 9, 1788
(5th state admitted)

Principal river
Connecticut River

Highest point
Mount Frissell; 2,380 feet
(725 m.)

Largest city
Bridgeport (141,686 people)

Motto
Qui transtulit sustinet (He
who transplanted still
sustains)

Song
"Yankee Doodle"

Famous people
Ethan Allen, P.T. Barnum,
Katharine Hepburn, Harriet
Beecher Stowe

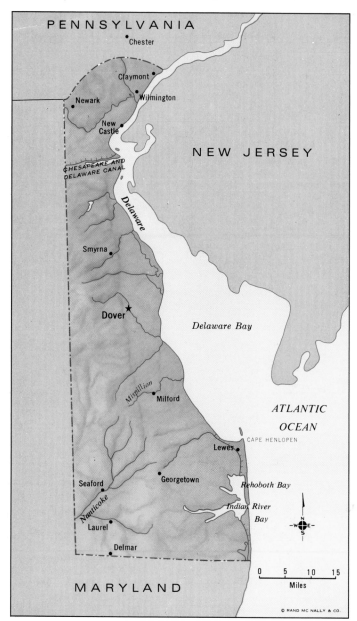

Wilmington contains several historic and lovely buildings, including the Grand Opera House, shown here.

DELAWARE

Capital
Dover (27,630 people)
Area
1,933 square miles (5,006 sq. km.)
Rank: 49th
Population
668,696 people Rank: 46th
Statehood
Dec. 7, 1787 (1st state admitted)
Principal river Delaware River
Highest point
442 feet (135 m.), in New Castle County
Largest city Wilmington (71,529 people)
Motto Liberty and independence
Song "Our Delaware"
Famous people
Thomas F. Bayard, John Dickinson, E.I. du Pont, Howard Pyle

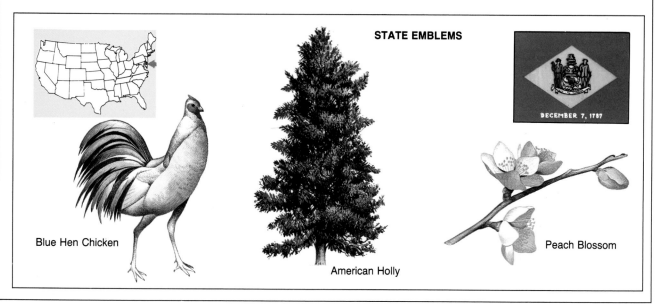

STATE EMBLEMS

Blue Hen Chicken

American Holly

Peach Blossom

DECEMBER 7, 1787

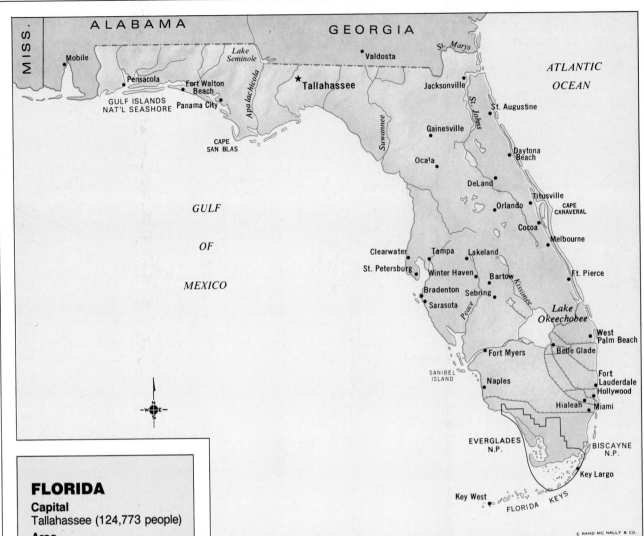

ALABAMA
GEORGIA
MISS.

Mobile
Pensacola
Fort Walton Beach
Panama City
GULF ISLANDS NAT'L SEASHORE
CAPE SAN BLAS
Lake Seminole
Tallahassee
Valdosta
St. Marys
Jacksonville
St. Augustine
Gainesville
Daytona Beach
Ocala
DeLand
Titusville
Orlando
CAPE CANAVERAL
Cocoa
Melbourne
Clearwater
Tampa
Lakeland
St. Petersburg
Winter Haven
Bartow
Ft. Pierce
Bradenton
Sebring
Sarasota
Lake Okeechobee
West Palm Beach
Fort Myers
Belle Glade
SANIBEL ISLAND
Naples
Fort Lauderdale
Hollywood
Hialeah
Miami
EVERGLADES N.P.
BISCAYNE N.P.
Key Largo
Key West
FLORIDA KEYS

Apalachicola
Suwannee
St. Johns
Kissimmee
Peace

ATLANTIC OCEAN

GULF

OF

MEXICO

© RAND MC NALLY & CO.

FLORIDA

Capital
Tallahassee (124,773 people)

Area
54,157 square miles
(140,266 sq. km.) Rank: 26th

Population
13,003,362 people Rank: 4th

Statehood
March 3, 1845 (27th state admitted)

Principal river
St. Johns River

Highest point
345 feet (105 m.), in Walton County

Largest city
Jacksonville (635,230 people)

Motto
In God we trust

Song
"Old Folks at Home"

Famous people
James Weldon Johnson, Ponce de León, Chris Evert, Sidney Poitier, A. Philip Randolph, Marjorie Kinnan Rawlings

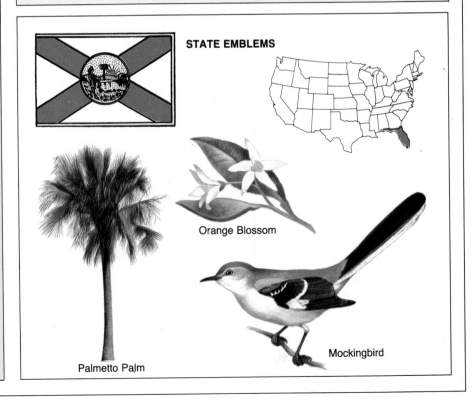

STATE EMBLEMS

Orange Blossom

Mockingbird

Palmetto Palm

TENNESSEE   N.C.

Chattanooga

Dalton

APPALACHIAN MTS.

Brasstown Bald
4 784 Ft.
1 458 M.

Greenville

Lake
Sidney Lanier

Hartwell
Lake

Rome

Gainesville

SOUTH
CAROLINA

Marietta

Athens

Atlanta   Decatur

Columbia

Carrollton

Chattahoochee

East Point

Clark
Hill
Lake

Griffin

Augusta

Milledgeville

Savannah

LaGrange

Macon

Oconee

Warner
Robbins

Statesboro

ALABAMA

Columbus

Savannah

Walter F.
George
Res.

Americus

Altamaha

Flint

Tifton

Chattahoochee

Albany

Moultree

Waycross

Brunswick

ST. SIMONS
ISLAND

ATLANTIC
OCEAN

Lake
Seminole

Thomasville

Valdosta

Okefenokee
Swamp

St. Marys

Jacksonville

N
W   E
S

0   25   50
Miles

FLORIDA

© RAND MC NALLY & CO.

GEORGIA

Capital and largest city
Atlanta (394,017 people)

Area
58,060 square miles (150,375 sq. km.) Rank: 21st

Population
6,508,419 people Rank: 11th

Statehood
Jan. 2, 1788 (4th state admitted)

Principal rivers
Chattahoochee River, Flint River, Savannah River

Highest point
Brasstown Bald; 4,784 feet (1,458 m.)

Motto
Wisdom, justice and moderation

Song
"Georgia on My Mind"

Famous people
James Bowie, Erskine Caldwell, Jimmy Carter, Joel Chandler Harris, Martin Luther King, Jr., Sidney Lanier, Margaret Mitchell, Burt Reynolds

STATE EMBLEMS

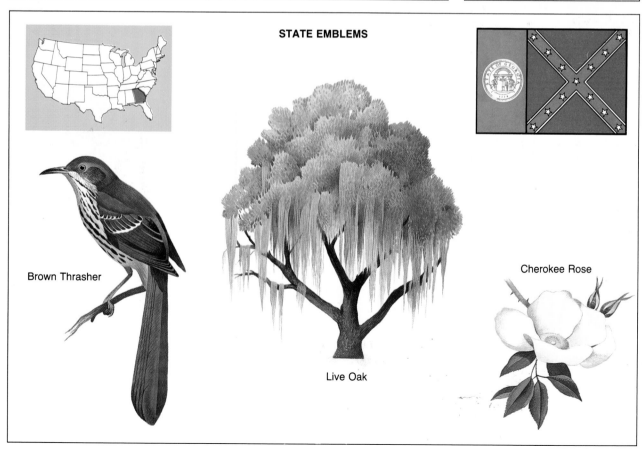

Brown Thrasher

Live Oak

Cherokee Rose

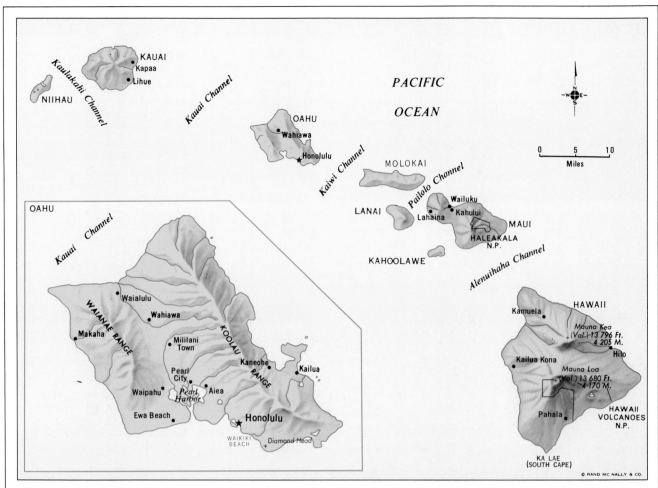

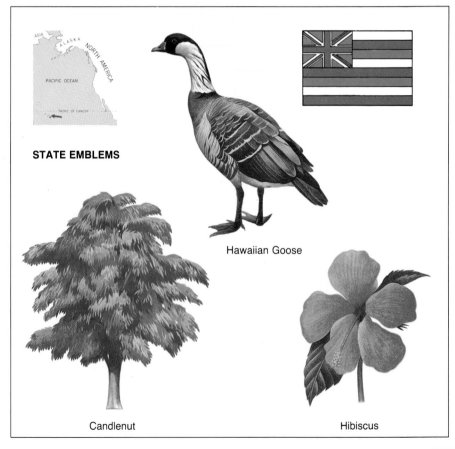

HAWAII

Capital and largest city
Honolulu (365,272 people)

Area
6,427 square miles (16,646 sq. km.) Rank: 47th

Population
1,115,274 people Rank: 40th

Statehood
Aug. 21, 1959 (50th state admitted)

Highest point
Mauna Kea; 13,796 feet (4,205 m.), on Hawaii

Motto
Ua mau ke ea o ka aina i ka pono (The life of the land is perpetuated in righteousness)

Song
"Hawaii Ponoi"

Famous people
Don Ho, Daniel K. Inouye, King Kamehameha, Bette Midler, Patsy Mink

STATE EMBLEMS

Hawaiian Goose

Candlenut

Hibiscus

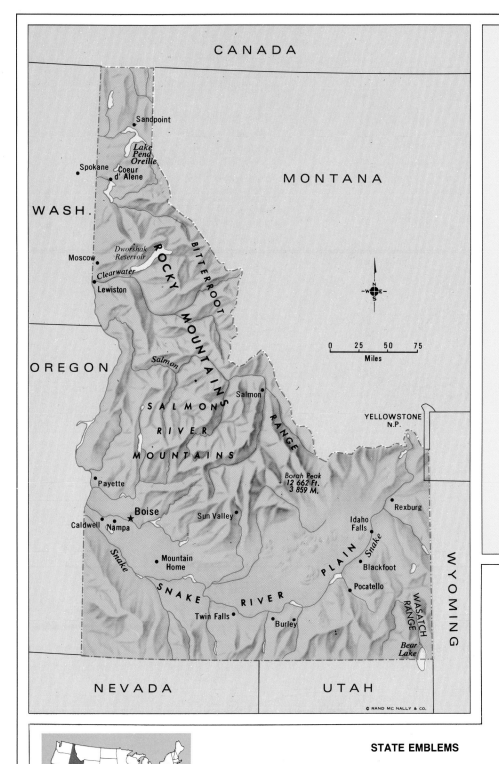

CANADA

MONTANA

WASH.

OREGON

NEVADA   UTAH

Sandpoint

Lake Pend Oreille

Spokane
Coeur d'Alene

Moscow
Dworshak Reservoir

Clearwater

Lewiston

ROCKY MOUNTAINS

BITTERROOT

Salmon

Salmon

SALMON RIVER MOUNTAINS

RANGE

YELLOWSTONE N.P.

Payette

Borah Peak 12 662 Ft. 3 859 M.

Boise

Caldwell Nampa

Sun Valley

Mountain Home

Rexburg

Idaho Falls

Snake

Blackfoot

Pocatello

Twin Falls   Burley

SNAKE   RIVER   PLAIN

WASATCH RANGE

Snake

WYOMING

Bear Lake

© RAND MC NALLY & CO.

0   25   50   75
Miles

IDAHO

Capital and largest city
Boise (125,738 people)

Area
82,413 square miles
(213,449 sq. km.)
Rank: 11th

Population
1,011,986 people
Rank: 42st

Statehood
July 3, 1890 (43rd state
admitted)

Principal river
Snake River

Highest point
Borah Peak; 12,662 feet
(3,859 m.)

Motto
Esto perpetua (Let it be
perpetual)

Song
''Here We Have Idaho''

Famous people
Moses Alexander,
William Borah, Gutzon
Borglum, Frank Church,
Ezra Pound

STATE EMBLEMS

Mountain Bluebird

Idaho Syringa

White Pine

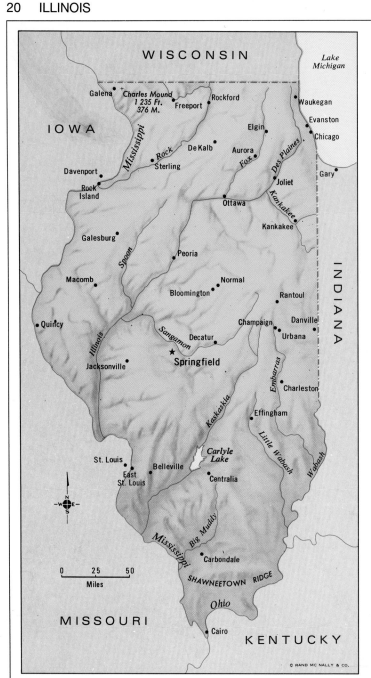

ILLINOIS

Capital
Springfield (105,227 people)

Area
55,646 square miles (144,122 sq. km.)
Rank: 24th

Population
11,466,682 people Rank: 6th

Statehood
Dec. 3, 1818 (21st state admitted)

Principal rivers
Illinois River, Mississippi River, Ohio River

Highest point
Charles Mound; 1,235 feet (376 m.)

Largest city
Chicago (2,783,726 people)

Motto
State sovereignty-national union

Song
''Illinois''

Famous people
Jane Addams, Walt Disney, Ulysses S. Grant, Jesse Jackson, Abraham Lincoln, Carl Sandburg

Historic Galena was once Illinois's leading city. Today, Chicago is.

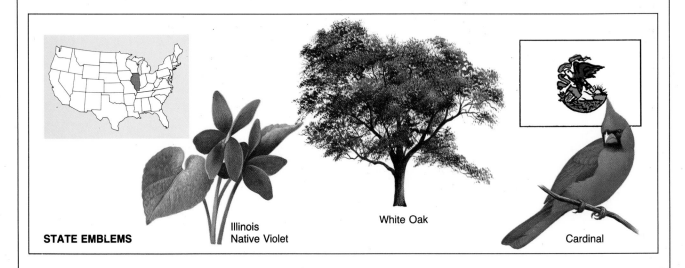

STATE EMBLEMS

Illinois
Native Violet

White Oak

Cardinal

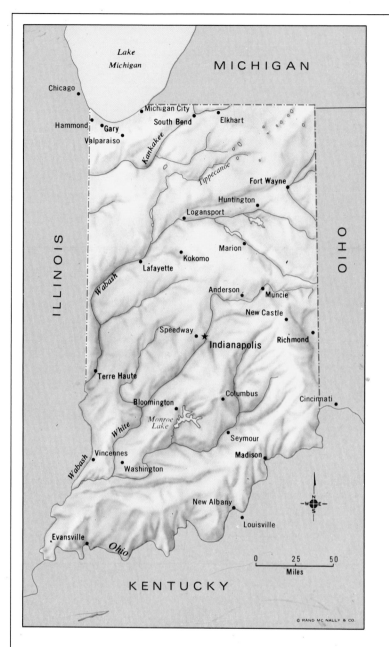

INDIANA

Capital and largest city
Indianapolis (731,327 people)

Area
35,936 square miles (93,074 sq. km.)
Rank: 38th

Population
5,564,228 people Rank: 14th

Statehood
Dec. 11, 1816 (19th state admitted)

Principal rivers
Ohio River, Wabash River

Highest point
1,257 feet (383 m.), in Wayne County

Motto
Crossroads of America

Song
"On the Banks of the Wabash, Far Away"

Famous people
Hoagy Carmichael, Theodore Dreiser, Michael Jackson, Cole Porter, Ernie Pyle, Booth Tarkington

This covered bridge is one of the sights of rural Indiana.

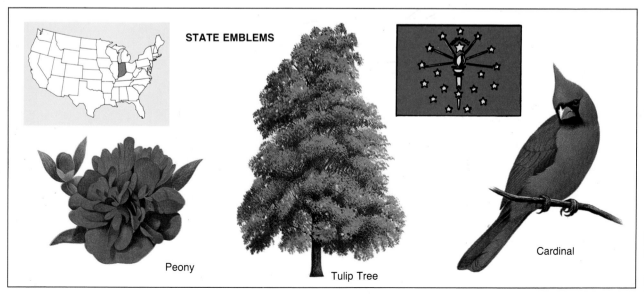

STATE EMBLEMS

Peony

Tulip Tree

Cardinal

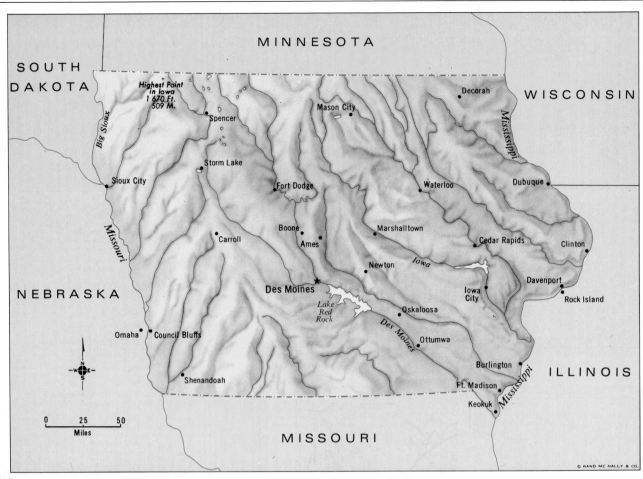

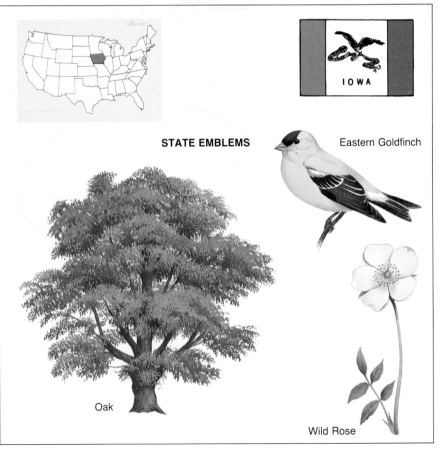

IOWA

Capital and largest city
Des Moines (193,187 people)

Area
55,965 square miles (144,949 sq. km.) Rank: 23rd

Population
2,787,424 people Rank: 30th

Statehood
Dec. 28, 1846 (29th state admitted)

Principal rivers
Des Moines River, Mississippi River, Missouri River

Highest point
1,670 feet (509 m.), in Osceola County

Motto
Our liberties we prize and our rights we will maintain

Song
"The Song of Iowa"

Famous people
James Van Allen, "Buffalo Bill" Cody, Herbert Hoover, John Wayne, Grant Wood

STATE EMBLEMS

Eastern Goldfinch

Oak

Wild Rose

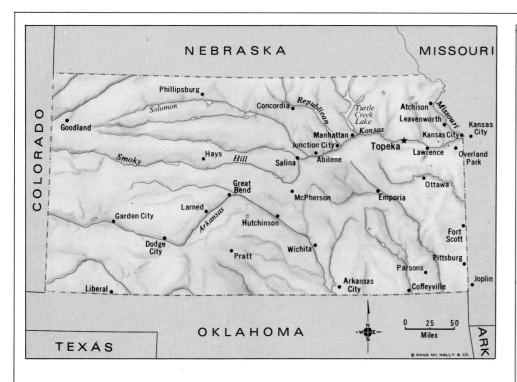

KANSAS

Capital
Topeka (119,883 people)

Area
81,783 square miles
(211,817 sq. km.)
Rank: 13th

Population
2,485,600 people
Rank: 32nd

Statehood
Jan. 29, 1861 (34th
state admitted)

Principal rivers
Arkansas River, Kansas
River

Highest point
Mount Sunflower; 4,039
feet (1,231 m.)

Largest city
Wichita (304,011 people)

Motto
Ad astra per aspera (To
the stars through
difficulties)

Song
"Home on the Range"

Famous people
Thomas Hart Benton,
Amelia Earhart, Dwight
D. Eisenhower, Carry
Nation, William Allen
White

STATE EMBLEMS

Cottonwood

Western Meadowlark

Sunflower

Kansas City is an
important junction
of rail, highway,
and water routes.

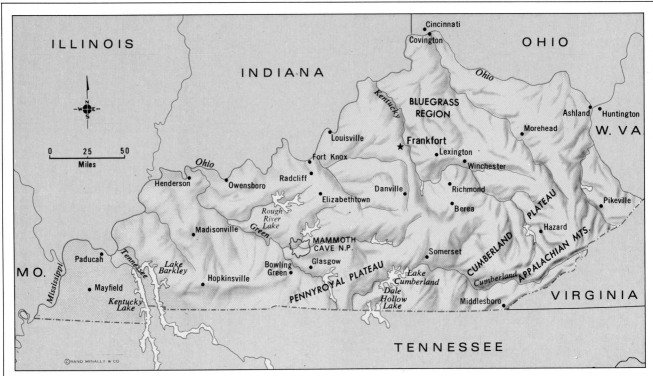

KENTUCKY

Capital
Frankfort (25,968 people)

Area
39,674 square miles (102,755 sq. km.) Rank: 37th

Population
3,698,969 people Rank: 23rd

Statehood
June 1, 1792 (15th state admitted)

Principal rivers
Cumberland River, Kentucky River, Ohio River

Highest point
Black Mountain; 4,139 feet (1,262 m.)

Largest city
Louisville (269,063 people)

Motto
United we stand, divided we fall

Song
''My Old Kentucky Home''

Famous people
Muhammad Ali, John James Audubon, Daniel Boone, Loretta Lynn, Whitney M. Young

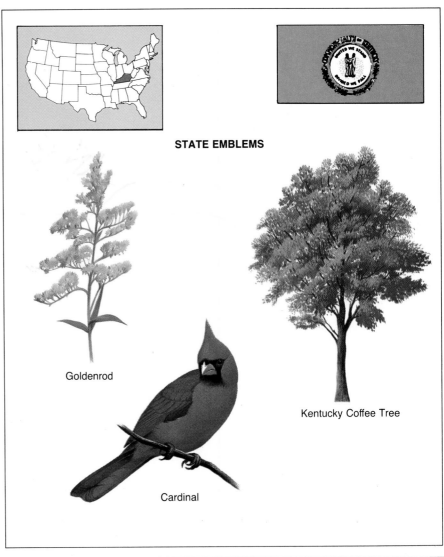

STATE EMBLEMS

Goldenrod

Kentucky Coffee Tree

Cardinal

© RAND MC NALLY & CO.

LOUISIANA

Capital
Baton Rouge (219,531 people)

Area
44,520 square miles (115,306 sq. km.)
Rank: 33rd

Population
4,238,216 people
Rank: 21st

Statehood
April 30, 1812 (18th state admitted)

Principal rivers
Mississippi River, Red River, Sabine River

Highest point
Driskill Mountain; 535 feet (163 m.)

Largest city
New Orleans (496,938 people)

Motto
Union, justice, and confidence

Song
"Give Me Louisiana"

Famous people
Louis Armstrong, Pierre Beauregard, Lillian Hellman, Mahalia Jackson, Huey Long

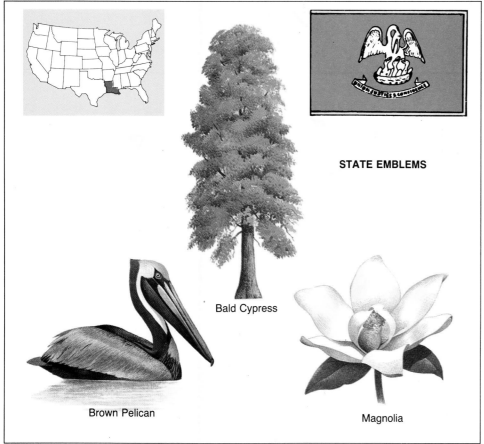

STATE EMBLEMS

Bald Cypress

Brown Pelican

Magnolia

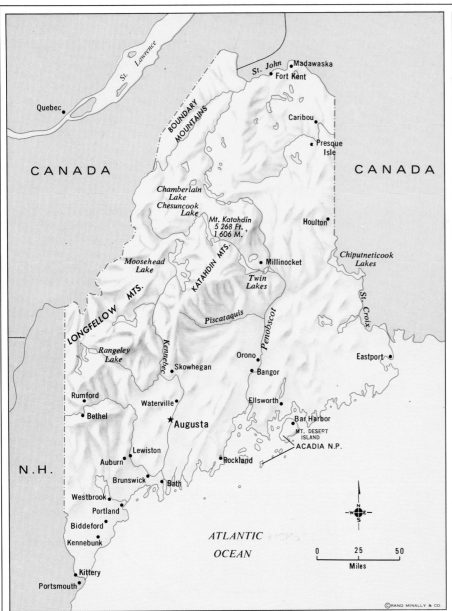

MAINE

Capital
Augusta (21,325 people)

Area
30,995 square miles (80,277 sq. km.) Rank: 39th

Population
1,233,223 people
Rank: 38th

Statehood
March 15, 1820 (23rd state admitted)

Principal river
Penobscot River

Highest point
Mount Katahdin; 5,268 feet (1,606 m.)

Largest city
Portland (64,358 people)

Motto
Dirigo (I direct)

Song
"State of Maine Song"

Famous people
Hannibal Hamlin, Henry Wadsworth Longfellow, Sir Hiram Maxim, Edna St. Vincent Millay

STATE EMBLEMS

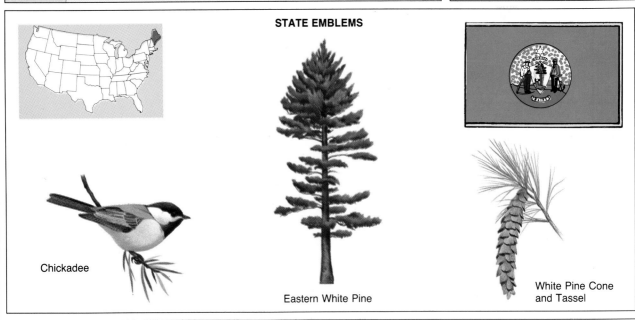

Chickadee

Eastern White Pine

White Pine Cone and Tassel

MARYLAND

Capital
Annapolis (33,187 people)

Area
9,838 square miles (25,480 sq. km.) Rank: 42nd

Population
4,798,622 people Rank: 19th

Statehood
April 28, 1788 (7th state admitted)

Principal rivers
Patuxent River, Potomac River

Highest point
Backbone Mountain; 3,360 feet (1,024 m.)

Largest city
Baltimore (736,014 people)

Motto
Fatti maschii, parole femine (Manly deeds, womanly words)

Song
''Maryland, My Maryland''

Famous people
Benjamin Banneker, Frederick Douglas, Francis Scott Key, George Herman (''Babe'') Ruth, Upton Sinclair

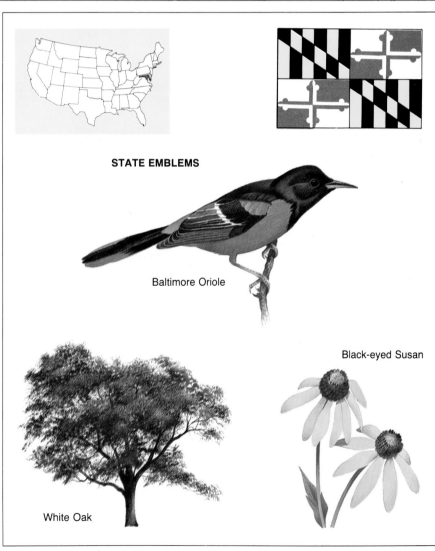

STATE EMBLEMS

Baltimore Oriole

Black-eyed Susan

White Oak

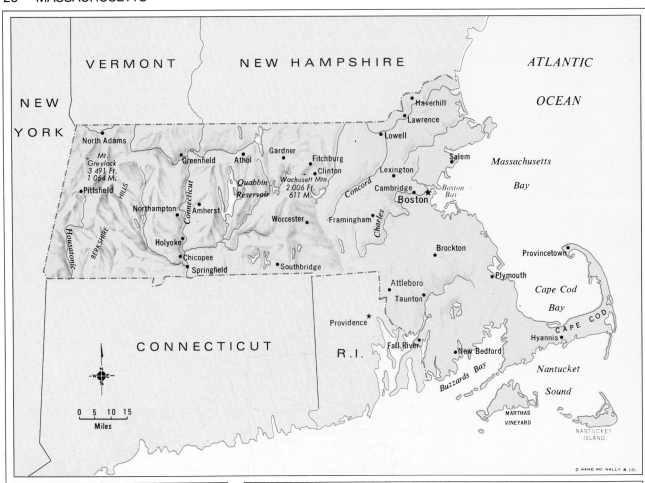

MASSACHUSETTS

Capital and largest city
Boston (574,283 people)

Area
7,826 square miles (20,269 sq. km.)
Rank: 45th

Population
6,029,051 people Rank: 13th

Statehood
Feb. 6, 1788 (6th state admitted)

Principal river
Connecticut River

Highest point
Mount Greylock; 3,491 feet
(1,064 m.)

Motto
*Ense petit placidam sub libertate
quietem* (By the sword we seek
peace, but peace only under liberty)

Song
"All Hail to Massachusetts"

Famous people
John Adams, John Quincy Adams,
Louisa May Alcott, Leonard
Bernstein, Emily Dickinson, Ralph
Waldo Emerson, John F. Kennedy,
Horace Mann, Paul Revere

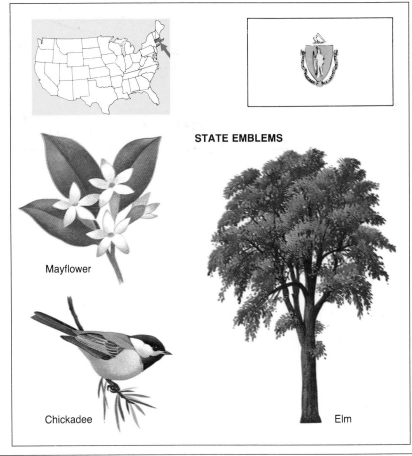

STATE EMBLEMS

Mayflower

Chickadee

Elm

MN.

ISLE ROYALE

LAKE SUPERIOR

CANADA

COPPER RANGE

KEWEENAW PEN.

Mt. Curwood
1 980 Ft.
604 M. • Ishpeming

• Marquette

Sault
Ste. Marie

DRUMMOND
ISLAND

• Ironwood

Iron Mountain

• Manistique

Straits of Mackinac

Mackinaw
City

LAKE HURON

BEAVER ISLANDS

• Petoskey

Green Bay

Alpena •

Menominee •

• Traverse City Grayling

WISCONSIN

LAKE MICHIGAN

• Manistee

• Cadillac
Ludington • Marion

Saginaw Bay

Muskegon

• Muskegon

Saginaw •

Flint •

Port Huron •

Milwaukee •

• Grand Rapids

Holland •

★ Lansing

Warren •

ILLINOIS

Kalamazoo • Kalamazoo

Livonia • Detroit •
Dearborn •

L. St.
Clair

Chicago •

Benton Harbor • Battle
Creek

Jackson • Ann Arbor • Windsor •

Monroe •

N
W E
S

0   50   100

Miles

INDIANA

Toledo •

OHIO

LAKE ERIE

© RAND MC NALLY & CO.

MICHIGAN

Capital
Lansing (127,321
people)

Area
56,959 square miles
(147,523 sq. km.)
Rank: 22nd

Population
9,328,784 people
Rank: 8th

Statehood
Jan. 26, 1837 (26th
state admitted)

Principal river
Muskegon River

Highest point
Mount Curwood;
1,980 feet (604 m.)

Largest city
Detroit (1,027,974
people)

Motto
*Si quaeris peninsulam
amoenam circumspice*
(If you seek a
pleasant peninsula,
look about you)

Song
"Michigan, My
Michigan"

Famous people
George Custer,
Thomas Dewey, Edna
Ferber, Henry Ford,
Robert Jarvik

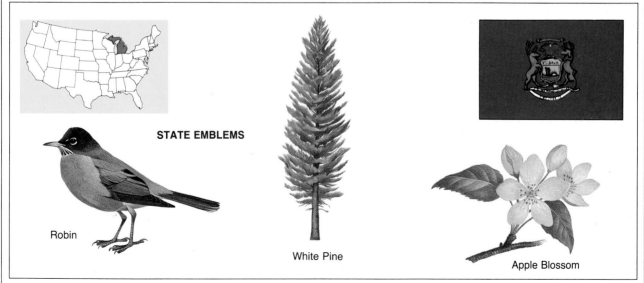

STATE EMBLEMS

Robin

White Pine

Apple Blossom

Situated near the head of the Mississippi River, Minneapolis and St. Paul are a center for business and culture in the northern Midwest.

MINNESOTA

Capital
St. Paul (272,235 people)

Area
79,548 square miles (206,028 sq. km.) Rank: 14th

Population
4,387,029 people Rank: 20th

Statehood
May 11, 1858 (32nd state admitted)

Principal rivers
Mississippi River, Red River

Highest point
Eagle Mountain; 2,301 feet (701 m.)

Largest city
Minneapolis (368,383 people)

Motto
L'Etoile du nord (The north star)

Song
"Hail! Minnesota"

Famous people
F. Scott Fitzgerald, Hubert Humphrey, Sinclair Lewis, Walter Mondale, Charles Schulz

STATE EMBLEMS

Common Loon

Red Pine

Pink-and-white Lady's Slipper

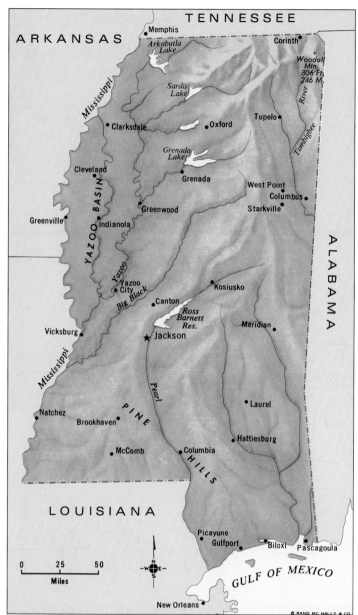

MISSISSIPPI

Capital and largest city
Jackson (196,637 people)

Area
47,234 square miles (122,335 sq. km.)
Rank: 31st

Population
2,586,443 people Rank: 31st

Statehood
Dec. 10, 1817 (20th state admitted)

Principal rivers
Mississippi River, Pearl River

Highest point
Woodall Mountain; 806 feet (246 m.)

Motto
Virtute et armis (By valor and arms)

Song
"Go, Mississippi"

Famous people
Jefferson Davis, William Faulkner, Elvis Presley, Leontyne Price, Eudora Welty, Tennessee Williams

Tourists can still ride steamboats up and down the Mississippi River.

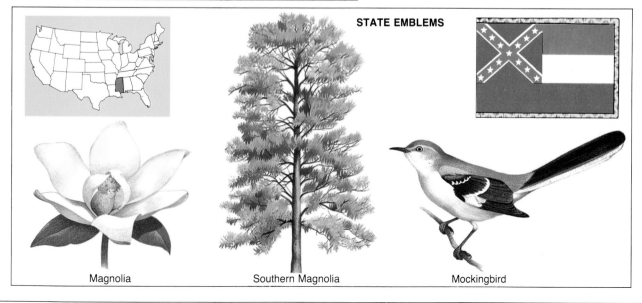

STATE EMBLEMS

Magnolia

Southern Magnolia

Mockingbird

MISSOURI

Capital
Jefferson City (35,481 people)

Area
68,945 square miles (178,567 sq. km.)
Rank: 18th

Population
5,137,804 people
Rank: 15th

Statehood
Aug. 10, 1821 (24th state admitted)

Principal rivers
Mississippi River,
Missouri River

Highest point
Taum Sauk Mountain;
1,772 feet (540 m.)

Largest city
Kansas City (435,146 people)

Motto
Salus populi suprema lex esto (The welfare of the people shall be the supreme law)

Song
"Missouri Waltz"

Famous people
Thomas Hart Benton, George Washington Carver, Samuel Clemens (Mark Twain), Joseph Pulitzer, Harry S Truman

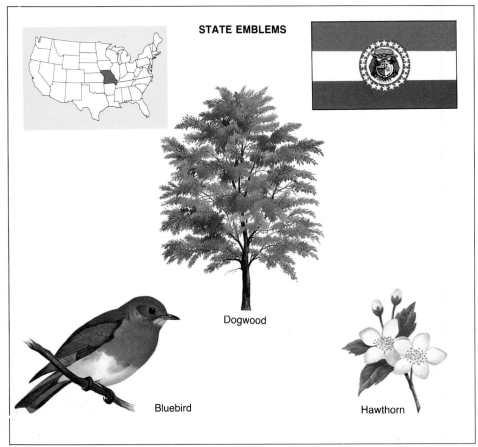

STATE EMBLEMS

Dogwood

Bluebird

Hawthorn

The Law Courts at St. Louis framed by the Gateway to the West.

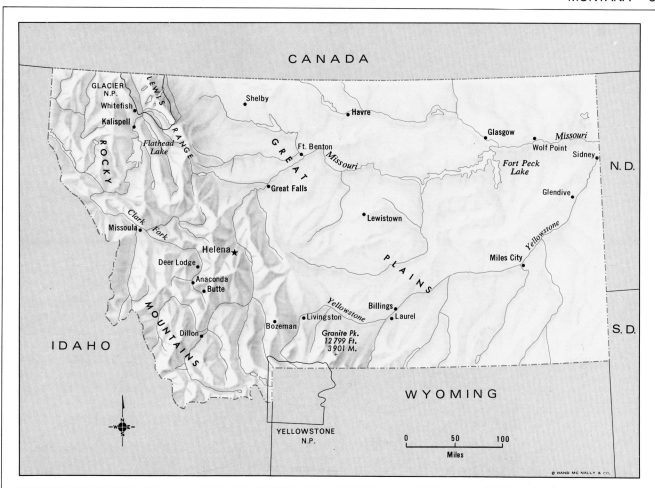

MONTANA

Capital
Helena (24,569 people)

Area
145,388 square miles
(376,553 sq. km.) Rank: 4th

Population
803,655 people Rank: 44th

Statehood
Nov. 8, 1889 (41st state
admitted)

Principal rivers
Missouri River, Yellowstone
River

Highest point
Granite Peak; 12,799 feet
(3,901 m.)

Largest city
Billings (81,151 people)

Motto
Oro y plata (Gold and silver)

Song
"Montana"

Famous people
Gary Cooper, Will James,
Mike Mansfield, Jeannette
Rankin, Charles Russell

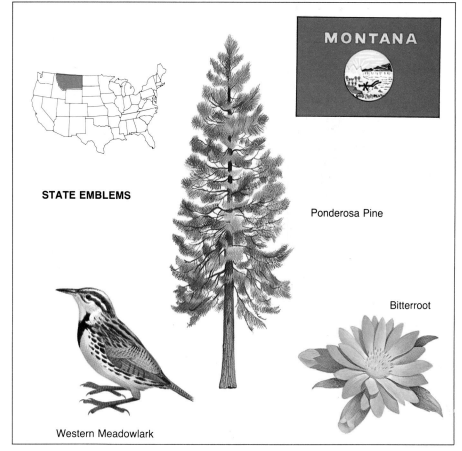

STATE EMBLEMS

Ponderosa Pine

Bitterroot

Western Meadowlark

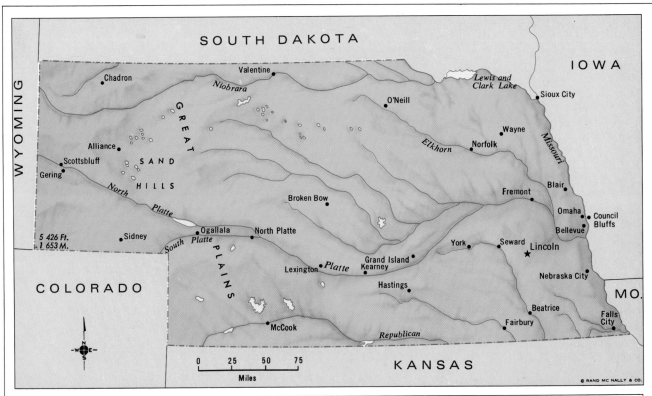

NEBRASKA

Capital
Lincoln (191,972 people)

Area
76,639 square miles (198,494 sq. km.) Rank: 15th

Population
1,584,617 people Rank: 36th

Statehood
March 1, 1867 (37th state admitted)

Principal rivers
Missouri River, Platte River

Highest point
5,426 feet (1,654 m.), in Kimball County

Largest city
Omaha (335,795 people)

Motto
Equality before the law

Song
"Beautiful Nebraska"

Famous people
Fred Astaire, Willa Cather, Johnny Carson, Henry Fonda, Gerald R. Ford, Malcolm X

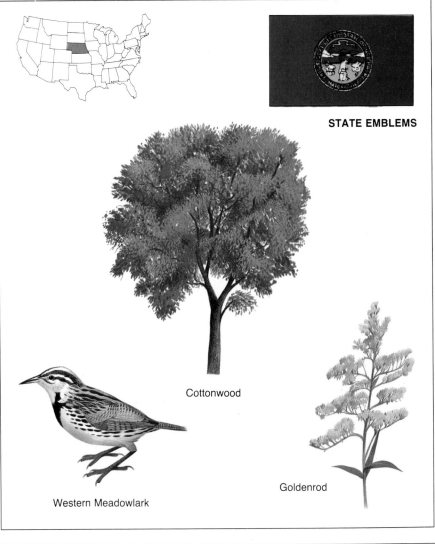

STATE EMBLEMS

Cottonwood

Goldenrod

Western Meadowlark

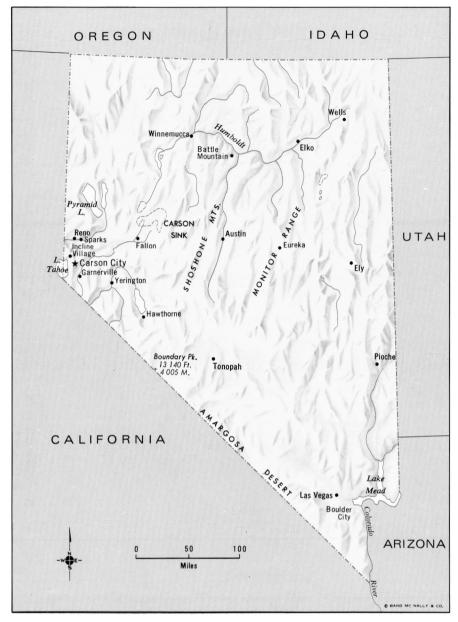

OREGON

IDAHO

Wells

Winnemucca
Humboldt
Battle
Mountain
Elko

Pyramid
L.

CARSON
SINK

Reno
Sparks
Incline
Village
L.
Tahoe
Carson City
Garnerville
Yerington
Fallon

Austin

SHOSHONE MTS.

MONITOR RANGE

Eureka

Ely

UTAH

Hawthorne

Boundary Pk.
13 140 Ft.
4 005 M.
Tonopah

Pioche

CALIFORNIA

AMARGOSA DESERT

Lake
Mead

Las Vegas
Boulder
City

Colorado

ARIZONA

N
W E
S

0   50   100
Miles

River

© RAND MC NALLY & CO.

NEVADA

Capital
Carson City (40,443 people)

Area
109,895 square miles
(284,627 sq. km.) Rank: 7th

Population
1,206,152 people Rank: 39th

Statehood
Oct. 31, 1864 (36th state
admitted)

Principal rivers
Colorado River, Humboldt
River

Highest point
Boundary Peak; 13,140 feet
(4,005 m.)

Largest city
Las Vegas (258,295 people)

Motto
All for our country

Song
"Home Means Nevada"

Famous people
Patrick A. McCarran, Howard
R. Hughes, William M.
Stewart, George Wingfield,
Wovoka

STATE EMBLEMS

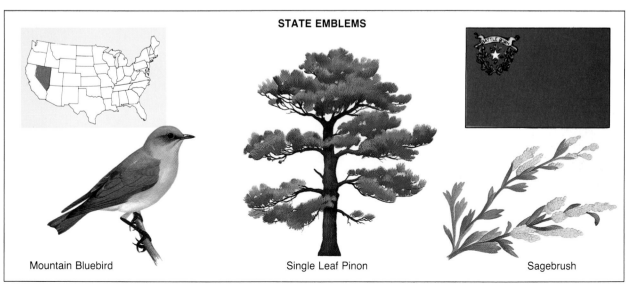

Mountain Bluebird

Single Leaf Pinon

Sagebrush

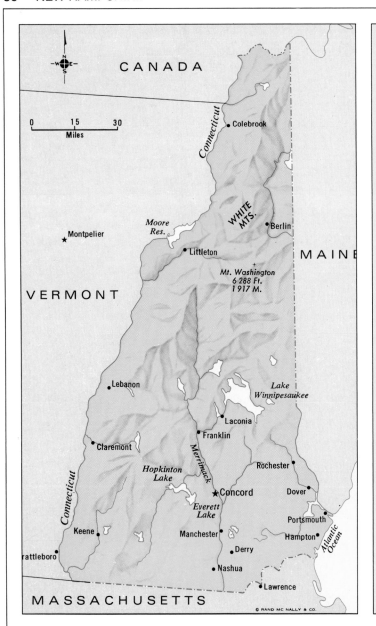

NEW HAMPSHIRE

Capital
Concord (36,006 people)

Area
8,992 square miles (23,289 sq. km.)
Rank: 44th

Population
1,113,915 people Rank: 41st

Statehood
June 21, 1788 (9th state admitted)

Principal rivers
Connecticut River, Merrimack River

Highest point
Mount Washington; 6,288 feet (1,917 m.)

Largest city
Manchester (99,567 people)

Motto
Live free or die

Song
"Old New Hampshire"

Famous people
Mary Baker Eddy, Robert Frost, Horace
Greeley, Franklin Pierce, Alan B. Shepard,
Jr., Daniel Webster

STATE EMBLEMS

Purple Finch

White Birch

Purple Lilac

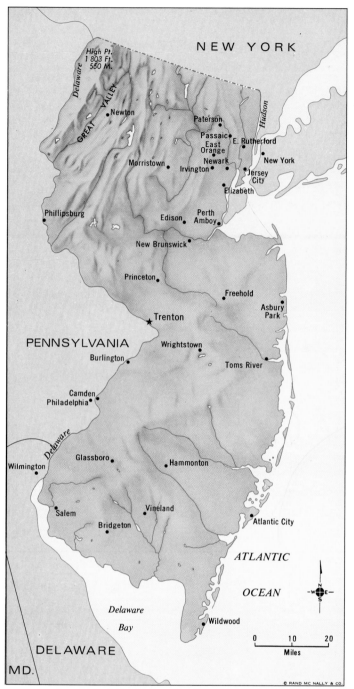

NEW YORK

High Pt.
1 803 Ft.
550 M.

Newton

Paterson

Passaic
East
Orange

E. Rutherford

Morristown

Newark

Irvington

New York

Jersey
City

Elizabeth

Phillipsburg

Edison

Perth
Amboy

New Brunswick

Princeton

Freehold

Asbury
Park

Trenton

PENNSYLVANIA

Wrightstown

Burlington

Toms River

Camden
Philadelphia

Glassboro

Hammonton

Wilmington

Salem

Vineland

Bridgeton

Atlantic City

ATLANTIC

OCEAN

Delaware
Bay

Wildwood

DELAWARE

MD.

0   10   20
Miles

© RAND MC NALLY & CO.

NEW JERSEY

Capital
Trenton (88,675 people)

Area
7,468 square miles (19,342 sq. km.)
Rank: 46th

Population
7,748,634 people Rank: 9th

Statehood
Dec. 18, 1787 (3rd state admitted)

Principal river
Delaware River

Highest point
High Point; 1,803 feet (550 m.)

Largest city
Newark (275,221 people)

Motto
Liberty and prosperity

Famous people
Count Basie, James Fenimore Cooper,
Thomas Edison, Albert Einstein, Molly Pitcher,
Paul Robeson, Frank Sinatra, Bruce
Springsteen, Walt Whitman

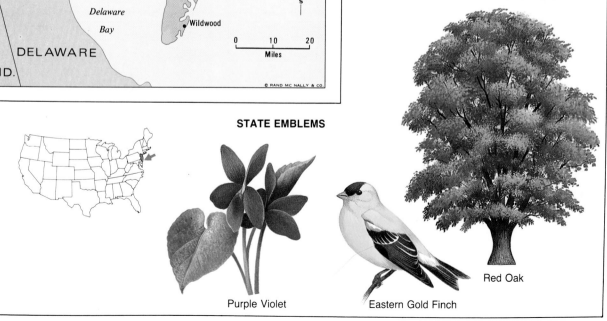

STATE EMBLEMS

Purple Violet

Eastern Gold Finch

Red Oak

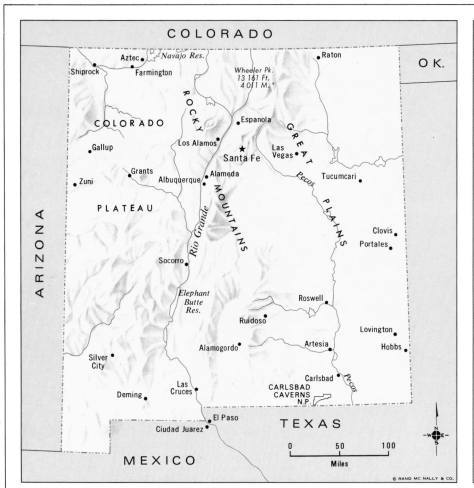

NEW MEXICO

Capital
Santa Fe (55,859 people)

Area
121,336 square miles
(314,259 sq. km.) Rank: 5th

Population
1,521,779 people
Rank: 37th

Statehood
Jan. 6, 1912 (47th state
admitted)

Principal rivers
Rio Grande, Pecos River

Highest point
Wheeler Peak; 13,161 feet
(4,011 m.)

Largest city
Albuquerque (384,736
people)

Motto
Crescit eundo (It grows as
it goes)

Song
"Asi es Nuevo Mexico" and
"O, Fair New Mexico"

Famous people
Kit Carson, Georgia
O'Keefe, Jean Baptiste
Lamy

STATE EMBLEMS

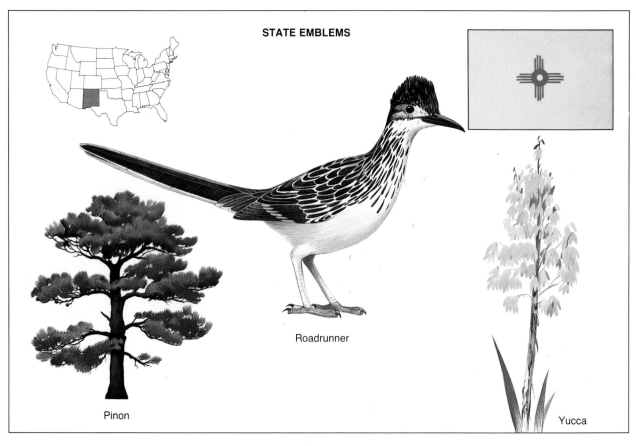

Pinon

Roadrunner

Yucca

NEW YORK

Capital
Albany (101,082 people)

Area
47,379 square miles (122,711 sq. km.) Rank: 30th

Population
18,044,505 people Rank: 2nd

Statehood
July 26, 1788 (11th state admitted)

Principal rivers
Hudson River, St. Lawrence River

Highest point
Mount Marcy; 5,344 feet (1,629 m.)

Largest city
New York (7,322,564 people)

Motto
Excelsior (Ever upward)

Song
"I Love New York"

Famous people
Woody Allen, George Gershwin, John Jay, Herman Melville, John D. Rockefeller, Franklin D. Roosevelt, Theodore Roosevelt, Jonas Salk

STATE EMBLEMS

Bluebird

Sugar Maple

Rose

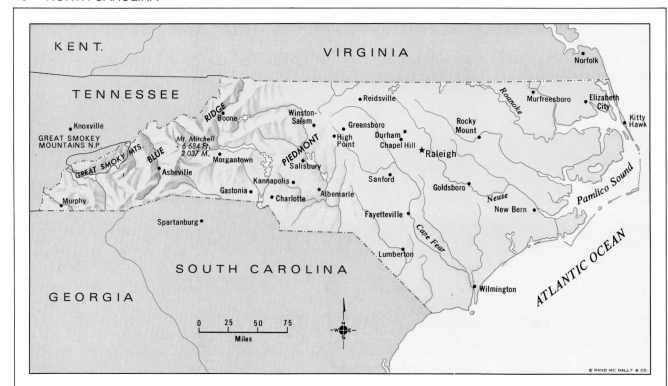

NORTH CAROLINA

Capital
Raleigh (207,951 people)

Area
48,843 square miles (126,503 sq. km.) Rank: 29th

Population
6,657,630 people Rank: 10th

Statehood
Nov. 21, 1789 (12th state admitted)

Principal rivers
Roanoke River, Neuse River, Cape Fear River

Highest point
Mount Mitchell; 6,684 feet (2,037 m.)

Largest city
Charlotte (395,934 people)

Motto
Esse quam videri (To be rather than to seem)

Song
"The Old North State"

Famous people
Virginia Dare, Billy Graham, Andrew Johnson, Dolley Madison, James K. Polk, Wilbur and Orville Wright

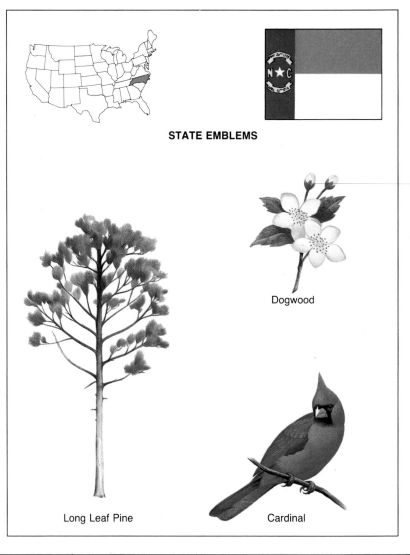

STATE EMBLEMS

Dogwood

Long Leaf Pine

Cardinal

NORTH DAKOTA

Capital
Bismarck (49,256 people)

Area
69,299 square miles (179,484 sq. km.)
Rank: 17th

Population
641,364 people
Rank: 47th

Statehood
Nov. 2, 1889 (39th state admitted)

Principal rivers
Missouri River, Red River

Highest point
White Butte; 3,506 feet (1,069 m.)

Largest city
Fargo (74,111 people)

Motto
Liberty and union, now and forever, one and inseparable

Song
"North Dakota Hymn"

Famous people
Louis L'Amour, Maxwell Anderson, Peggy Lee, Eric Severeid, Lawrence Welk

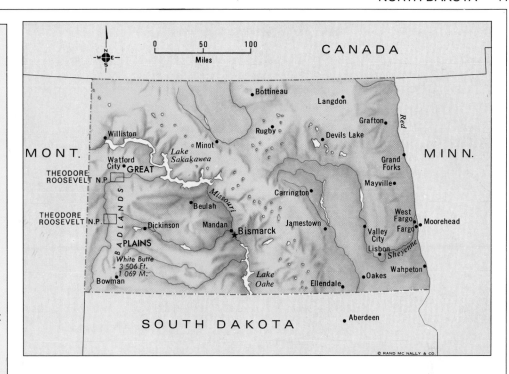

The valley of the Red River of the North is a rich agricultural region. The river flows north along the North Dakota–Minnesota border into Canada.

STATE EMBLEMS

Wild Prairie Rose

American Elm

Western Meadowlark

OHIO

Capital and largest city
Columbus (632,910 people)

Area
41,004 square miles (106,200 sq. km.)
Rank: 35th

Population
10,887,325 people
Rank: 7th

Statehood
March 1, 1803 (17th state admitted)

Principal rivers
Ohio River, Scioto River

Highest point
Campbell Hill; 1,550 feet (472 m.)

Motto
With God, all things are possible

Song
''Beautiful Ohio''

Famous people
Neil Armstrong, Thomas Edison, John Glenn, Steven Spielberg

STATE EMBLEMS

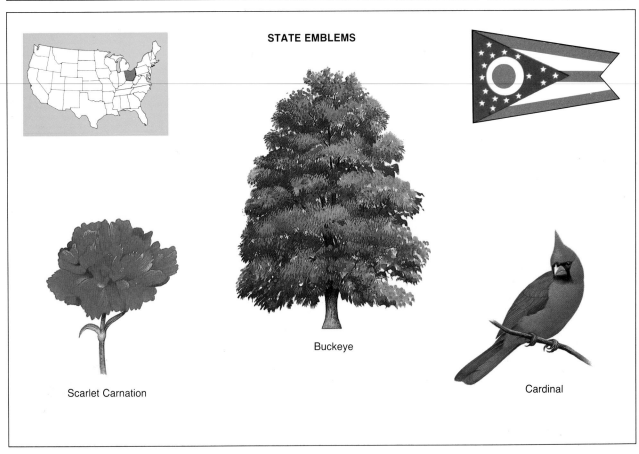

Scarlet Carnation

Buckeye

Cardinal

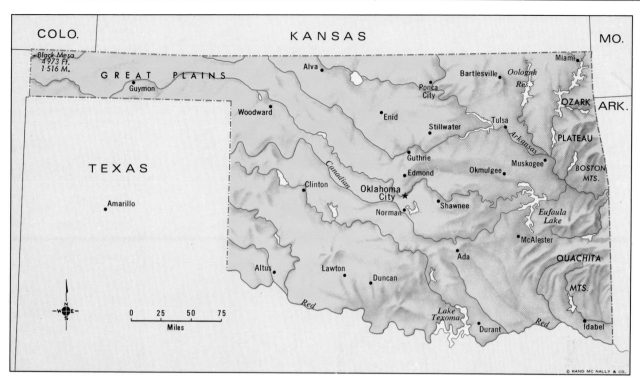

COLO.

KANSAS

MO.

Black Mesa
4,973 Ft.
1 516 M.

GREAT PLAINS

Miami

Guymon

Alva

Bartlesville

Oologah
Res.

OZARK

ARK.

Woodward

Ponca
City

Enid

Stillwater

Tulsa

Arkansas

PLATEAU

TEXAS

Guthrie

Edmond

Muskogee

BOSTON
MTS.

Okmulgee

Clinton

Oklahoma
City ★

Amarillo

Canadian

Shawnee

Eufaula
Lake

Norman

McAlester

Altus

Lawton

Ada

Duncan

OUACHITA

MTS.

Red

Lake
Texoma

Durant

Red

Idabel

N
W E
S

0   25   50   75
Miles

© RAND MC NALLY & CO.

OKLAHOMA

Capital and largest city
Oklahoma City (444,719 people)

Area
68,656 square miles (177,818 sq. km.)
Rank: 19th

Population
3,157,604 people Rank: 28th

Statehood
Nov. 16, 1907 (46th state admitted)

Principal rivers
Arkansas River, Canadian River, Red River

Highest point
Black Mesa; 4,973 feet (1,516 m.)

Motto
Labor omnia vincit (Labor conquers all things)

Song
"Oklahoma"

Famous people
Carl Albert, Woody Guthrie, Lynn Riggs, Oral Roberts, Will Rogers, Maria Tallchief, Jim Thorpe

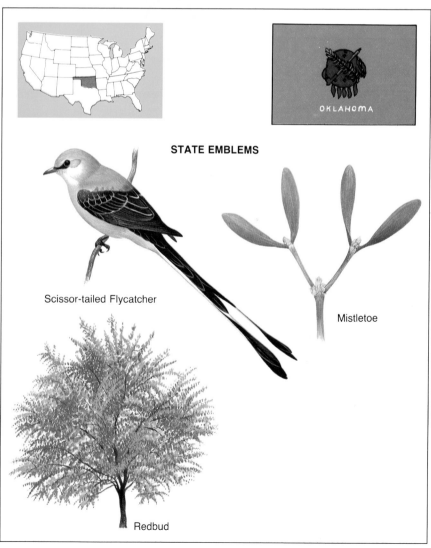

OKLAHOMA

STATE EMBLEMS

Scissor-tailed Flycatcher

Mistletoe

Redbud

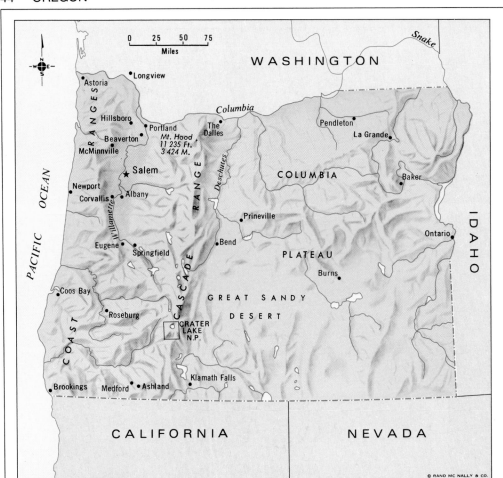

OREGON

Capital
Salem (107,786 people)

Area
96,187 square miles (249,123 sq. km.)
Rank: 10th

Population
2,853,733 people
Rank: 29th

Statehood
Feb. 14, 1859 (33rd state admitted)

Principal river
Columbia River

Highest point
Mount Hood; 11,235 feet (3,424 m.)

Largest city
Portland (437,319 people)

Motto
The Union

Song
"Oregon, My Oregon"

Famous people
Robert Gray, Chief Joseph, Linus Pauling

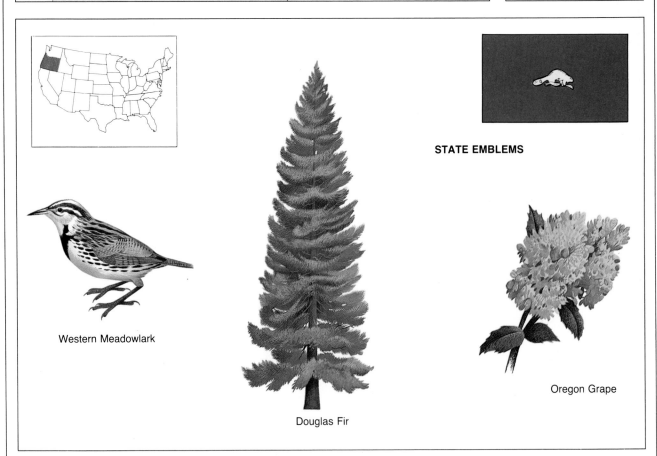

STATE EMBLEMS

Western Meadowlark

Douglas Fir

Oregon Grape

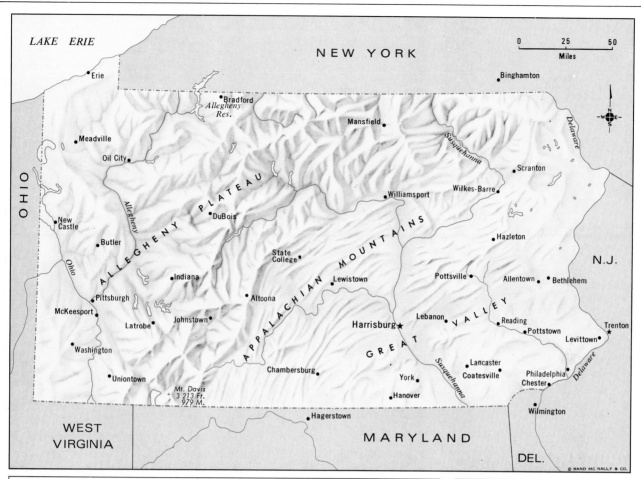

LAKE ERIE

NEW YORK

OHIO

WEST VIRGINIA

MARYLAND

DEL.

N.J.

Erie

Bradford
Allegheny Res.

Mansfield

Binghamton

Meadville

Oil City

Scranton

Williamsport

Wilkes-Barre

ALLEGHENY PLATEAU

DuBois

Hazleton

New Castle

State College

APPALACHIAN MOUNTAINS

Allentown

Bethlehem

Butler

Indiana

Lewistown

Pottsville

Pittsburgh

Altoona

Lebanon

Reading

Pottstown

Trenton

McKeesport

Latrobe

Johnstown

Harrisburg ★

GREAT VALLEY

Levittown

Washington

Chambersburg

Lancaster

Coatesville

Philadelphia

Chester

Uniontown

Mt. Davis 3,213 Ft. 979 M.

York

Hanover

Wilmington

Hagerstown

Susquehanna

Allegheny

Ohio

Delaware

Susquehanna

Delaware

0 25 50
Miles

© RAND MC NALLY & CO.

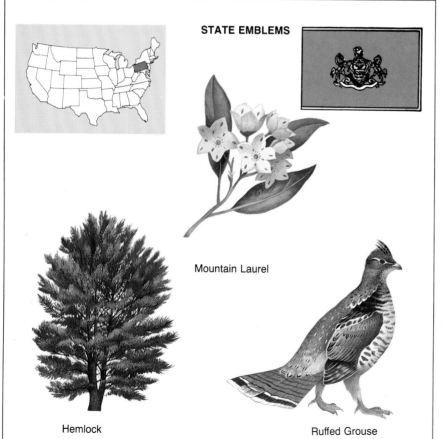

STATE EMBLEMS

Mountain Laurel

Hemlock

Ruffed Grouse

PENNSYLVANIA

Capital
Harrisburg (52,376 people)

Area
44,892 square miles (116,270 sq. km.) Rank: 32rd

Population
11,924,710 people Rank: 5th

Statehood
Dec. 12, 1787 (2nd state admitted)

Principal rivers
Allegheny River, Delaware River, Ohio River, Susquehanna River

Highest point
Mount Davis; 3,213 feet (979 m.)

Largest city
Philadelphia (1,585,577 people)

Motto
Virtue, liberty, and independence

Famous people
Andrew Carnegie, Bill Cosby, Stephen Foster, Martha Graham, Benjamin West

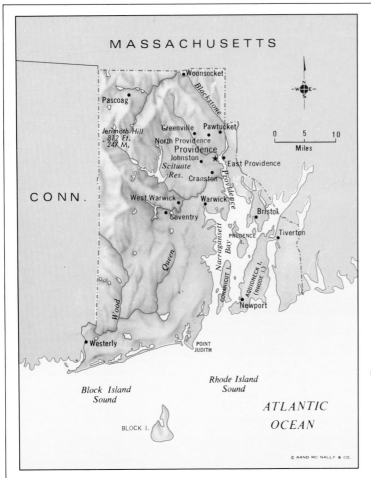

Historic Providence in one of New England's largest ports.

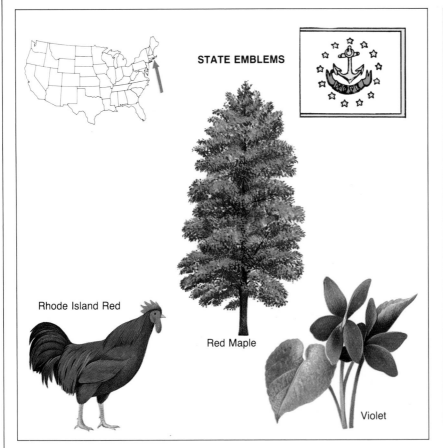

STATE EMBLEMS

Rhode Island Red

Red Maple

Violet

RHODE ISLAND

Capital and largest city
Providence (160,728 people)

Area
1,054 square miles (2,730 sq. km.) Rank: 50th

Population
1,005,984 people Rank: 43rd

Statehood
May 29, 1790 (13th state admitted)

Principal rivers
Blackstone River, Providence River

Highest point
Jerimoth Hill; 812 feet (247 m.)

Motto
Hope

Song
"Rhode Island"

Famous people
Ambrose Burnside, George M. Cohan, Nathanael Greene, Christopher and Oliver La Farge, Matthew C. and Oliver Perry, Gilbert Stuart

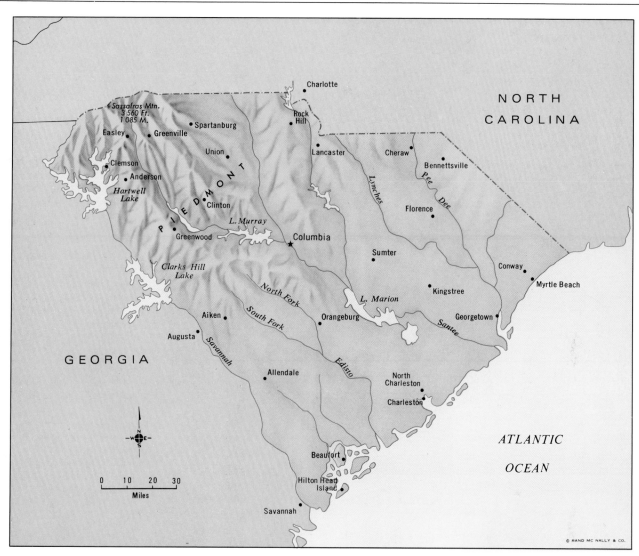

SOUTH CAROLINA

Capital and largest city
Columbia (99,052 people)

Area
30,207 square miles (78,236 sq. km.) Rank: 40th

Population
3,505,707 people Rank: 25th

Statehood
May 23, 1788 (8th state admitted)

Principal rivers
Savannah River, Pee Dee River

Highest point
Sassafras Mountain; 3,560 feet (1,085 m.)

Motto
Animis opibusque parati (Prepared in mind and resources) and *Dum spiro spero* (While I breathe, I hope)

Song
"South Carolina on My Mind"

Famous people
Mary McLeod Bethune, John C. Calhoun, Robert Mills

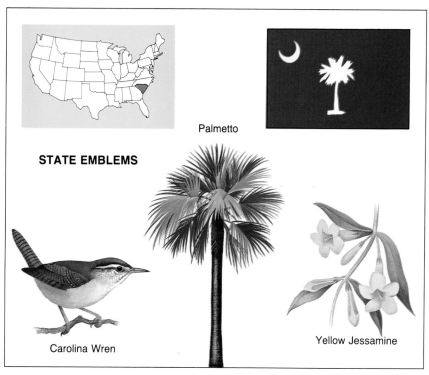

Palmetto

STATE EMBLEMS

Carolina Wren

Yellow Jessamine

SOUTH DAKOTA

Capital
Pierre (12,906 people)
Area
75,956 square miles
(196,725 sq. km.)
Rank: 16th
Population
699,999 people
Rank: 45th
Statehood
Nov. 2, 1889 (40th
state admitted)
Principal rivers
James River, Missouri
River
Highest point
Harney Peak; 7,242
feet (2,207 m.)
Largest city
Sioux Falls (100,814
people)
Motto
Under God the people
rule
Song
"Hail, South Dakota"
Famous people
Sitting Bull, Pierre
Chouteau, Jr., Crazy
Horse, Calamity Jane,
George McGovern,
Laura Ingalls Wilder

STATE EMBLEMS

Pasque Flower

Black Hills Spruce

Ring-necked Pheasant

The Badlands of southwestern South Dakota is a region of unusual rock formations created by erosion.

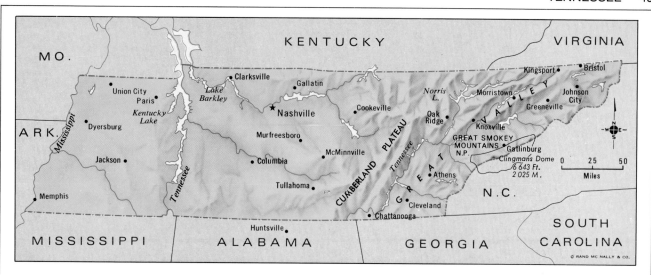

TENNESSEE

Capital
Nashville (487,969 people)

Area
41,154 square miles (106,588 sq. km.)
Rank: 34th

Population
4,896,641 people Rank: 17th

Statehood
June 1, 1796 (16th state admitted)

Principal rivers
Mississippi River, Tennessee River

Highest point
Clingmans Dome; 6,643 feet (2,025 m.)

Largest city
Memphis (610,337 people)

Motto
Agriculture and commerce

Song
"The Tennessee Waltz" and four others

Famous people
Davy Crockett, Dolly Parton

The Civil War cannon shown here overlooks Chattanooga at the Moccasin Bend of the Tennessee River.

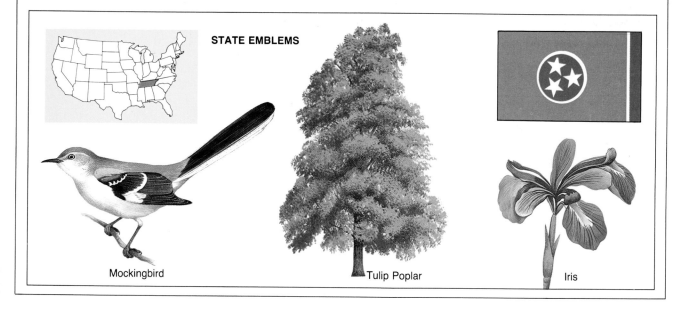

STATE EMBLEMS

Mockingbird

Tulip Poplar

Iris

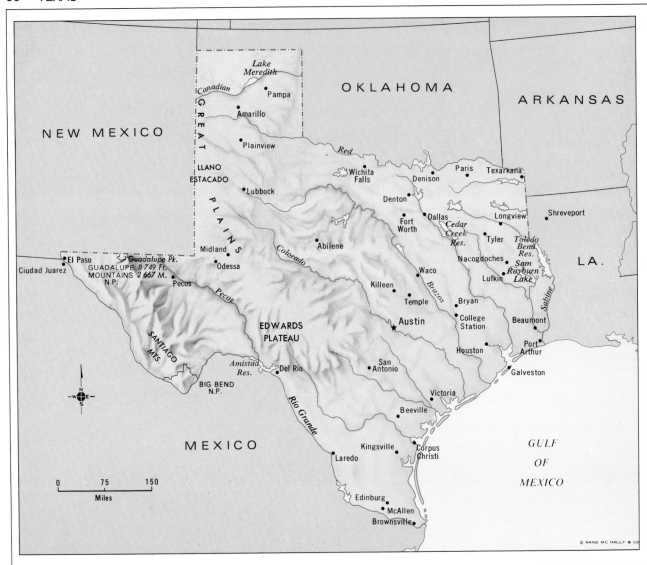

TEXAS

Capital
Austin (465,622 people)

Area
262,015 square miles (678,616 sq. km.) Rank: 2nd

Population
17,059,805 people Rank: 3rd

Statehood
Dec. 29, 1845 (28th state admitted)

Principal rivers
Pecos River, Red River, Rio Grande

Highest point
Guadalupe Peak; 8,749 feet (2,667 m.)

Largest city
Houston (1,630,553 people)

Motto
Friendship

Song
"Texas, Our Texas"

Famous people
Stephen Austin, Sam Houston, Lyndon B. Johnson, Willie Nelson

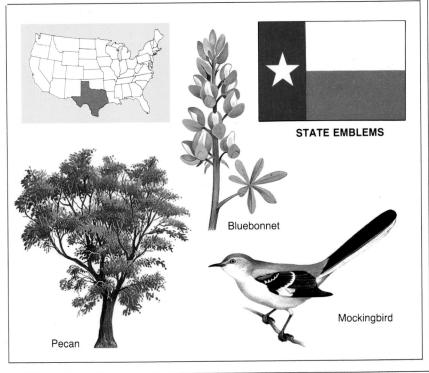

STATE EMBLEMS

Bluebonnet

Pecan

Mockingbird

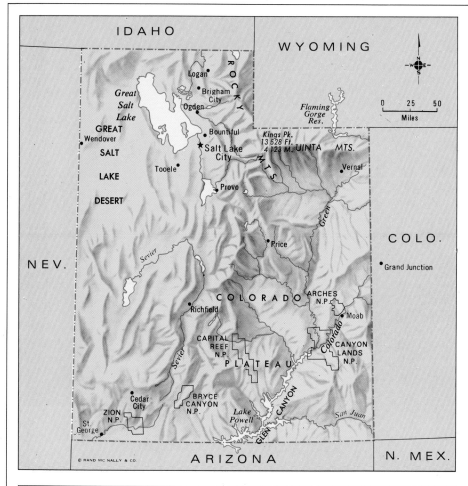

Temple Square in Salt Lake City features the Mormon Temple with its six granite spires.

STATE EMBLEMS

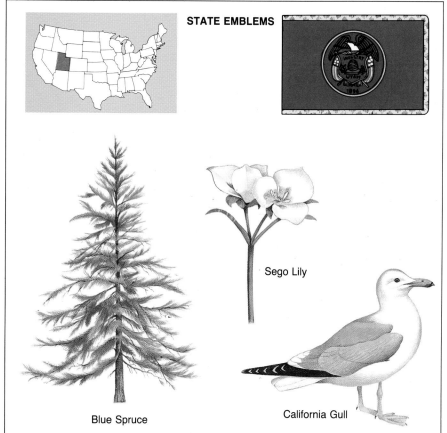

Sego Lily

Blue Spruce

California Gull

UTAH

Capital and largest city
Salt Lake City (159,936 people)

Area
82,076 square miles
(212,576 sq. km.)
Rank: 12th

Population
1,727,784 people
Rank: 35th

Statehood
Jan. 4, 1896 (45th state admitted)

Principal rivers
Colorado River, Green River

Highest point
Kings Peak; 13,528 feet
(4,123 m.)

Motto
Industry

Song
"Utah, We Love Thee"

Famous people
Maude Adams, John Moses Browning, Philo Farnsworth, the Osmond family, Brigham Young

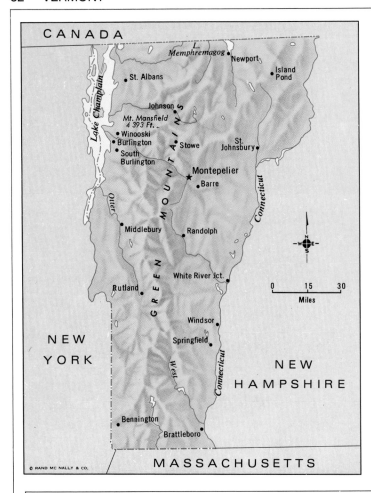

Autumn leaves line the roadside as walkers pass underneath a canopy of fall yellows in Vermont's scenic countryside.

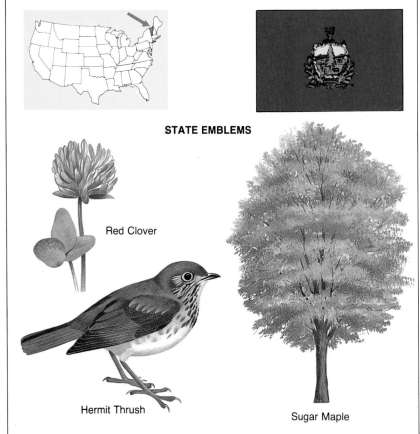

STATE EMBLEMS

Red Clover

Hermit Thrush

Sugar Maple

VERMONT

Capital
Montpelier (8,247 people)

Area
9,273 square miles (24,017 sq. km.) Rank: 43rd

Population
564,964 people Rank: 48th

Statehood
March 4, 1791 (14th state admitted)

Principal river
Connecticut River

Highest point
Mount Mansfield; 4,393 feet (1,339 m.)

Largest city
Burlington (39,127 people)

Motto
Freedom and unity

Song
"Hail, Vermont!"

Famous people
Ethan Allen, Chester Arthur, Calvin Coolidge, George Dewey, Stephen Douglas

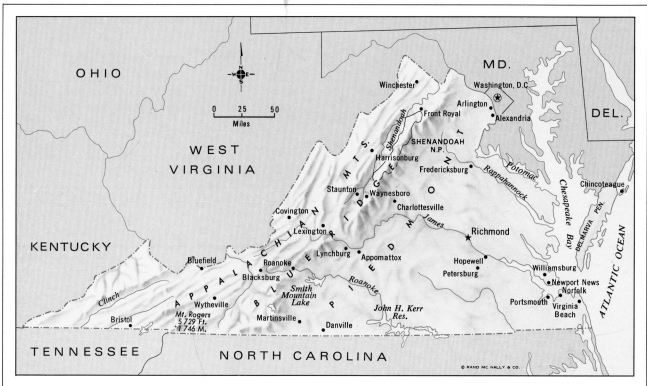

VIRGINIA

Capital
Richmond (203,056 people)

Area
39,700 square miles (102,823 sq. km.) Rank: 36th

Population
6,216,568 people Rank: 12th

Statehood
June 25, 1788 (10th state admitted)

Principal rivers
James River, Potomac River, Rappahannock River

Highest point
Mount Rogers; 5,729 feet (1,746 m.)

Largest city
Virginia Beach (393,069 people)

Motto
Sic semper tyrannis (Thus always to tyrants)

Song
"Carry Me Back to Old Virginia"

Famous people
Ella Fitzgerald, Patrick Henry, Thomas Jefferson, Robert E. Lee, James Madison, James Monroe, George C. Scott, John Tyler, Booker T. Washington, George Washington, Woodrow Wilson

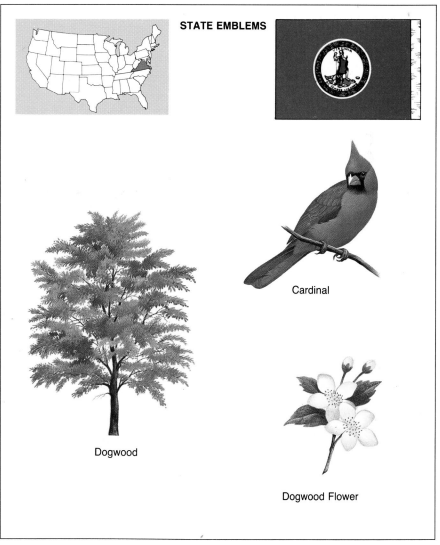

STATE EMBLEMS

Dogwood

Cardinal

Dogwood Flower

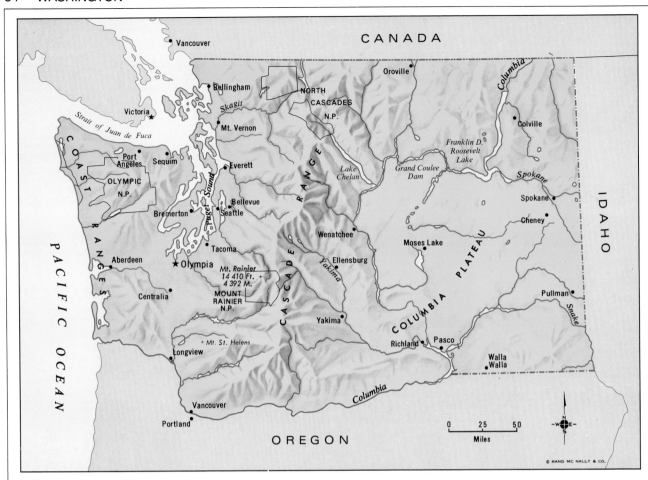

STATE EMBLEMS

Rhododendron

Western Hemlock

Willow Goldfinch

WASHINGTON

Capital
Olympia (33,840 people)

Area
66,512 square miles
(172,265 sq. km.)
Rank: 20th

Population
4,887,941 people
Rank: 18th

Statehood
Nov. 11, 1889 (42nd state
admitted)

Principal rivers
Columbia River, Snake River

Highest point
Mount Rainier; 14,410 feet
(4,392 m.)

Largest city
Seattle (516,259 people)

Motto
Alki (By and by)

Song
"Washington, My Home"

Famous people
Bing Crosby, William O.
Douglas, Mary McCarthy,
Dixie Lee Ray

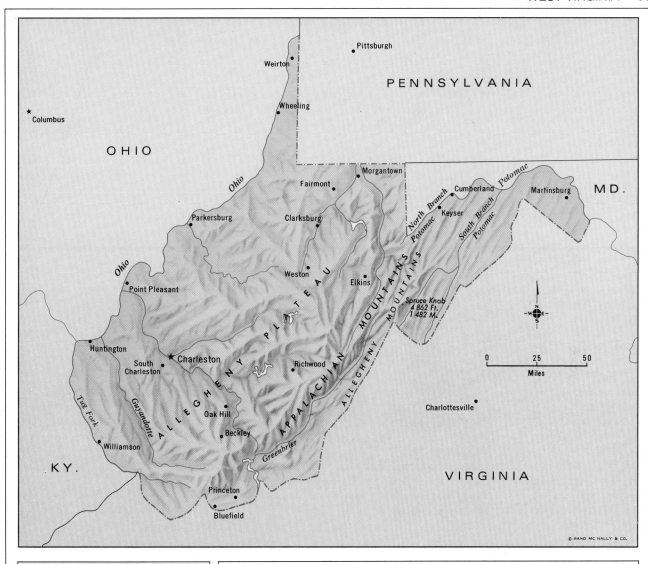

WEST VIRGINIA

Capital and largest city
Charleston (57,287 people)

Area
24,124 square miles (62,481 sq. km.) Rank: 41st

Population
1,801,625 people Rank: 34th

Statehood
June 20, 1863 (35th state admitted)

Principal river
Ohio River

Highest point
Spruce Knob; 4,862 feet (1,482 m.)

Motto
Montani semper liberi (Mountaineers are always free)

Song
"The West Virginia Hills" and two others

Famous people
Pearl Buck, Thomas "Stonewall" Jackson, Anna Jarvis

STATE EMBLEMS

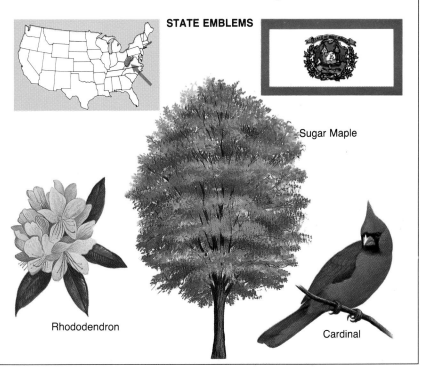

Sugar Maple

Rhododendron

Cardinal

Shown here is the capitol building of Wisconsin in Madison.

STATE EMBLEMS

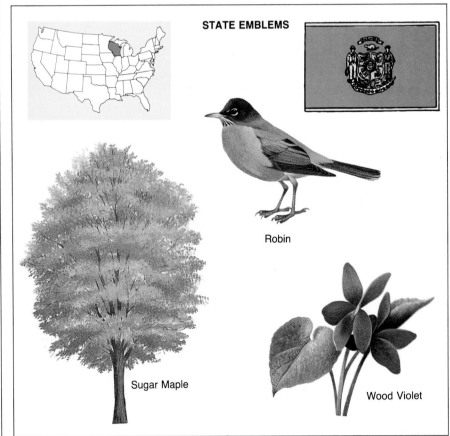

Robin

Sugar Maple

Wood Violet

WISCONSIN

Capital
Madison (191,262 people)

Area
54,424 square miles (140,958 sq. km.) Rank: 25th

Population
4,906,745 people Rank: 16th

Statehood
May 29, 1848 (30th state admitted)

Principal rivers
Mississippi River, Wisconsin River

Highest point
Timms Hill; 1,952 feet (595 m.)

Largest city
Milwaukee (628,088 people)

Motto
Forward

Song
"On, Wisconsin!"

Famous people
Harry Houdini, Robert La Follette, Jacques Marquette, Orson Welles, Thornton Wilder, Frank Lloyd Wright

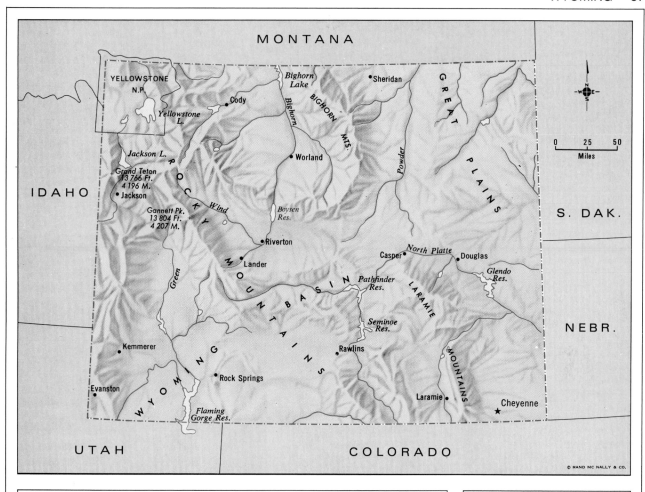

MONTANA

YELLOWSTONE N.P.

Yellowstone L.

Bighorn Lake

Sheridan

Cody

GREAT

BIGHORN MTS.

Bighorn

Worland

Powder

PLAINS

IDAHO

Jackson L.

Grand Teton 13 766 Ft. 4 196 M.

Jackson

Wind

Gannett Pk. 13 804 Ft. 4 207 M.

Boysen Res.

S. DAK.

ROCKY

Riverton

Lander

Green

North Platte

Casper

Douglas

Glendo Res.

Pathfinder Res.

LARAMIE

NEBR.

MOUNTAINS

BASIN

Seminoe Res.

WYOMING

Kemmerer

Rawlins

MOUNTAINS

Rock Springs

Laramie

Evanston

Cheyenne

Flaming Gorge Res.

UTAH

COLORADO

0 25 50
Miles

© RAND MC NALLY & CO.

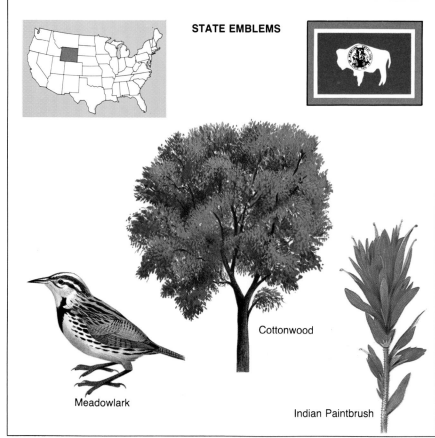

STATE EMBLEMS

Cottonwood

Meadowlark

Indian Paintbrush

WYOMING

Capital and largest city
Cheyenne (50,008 people)

Area
96,988 square miles (251,198 sq. km.) Rank: 9th

Population
455,975 people Rank: 50th

Statehood
July 10, 1890 (44th state admitted)

Principal rivers
Bighorn River, Green River, North Platte River

Highest point
Gannett Peak; 13,804 feet (4,207 m.)

Motto
Equal rights

Song
"Wyoming"

Famous people
"Buffalo Bill" Cody, Esther Morris, Nellie Tayloe Ross

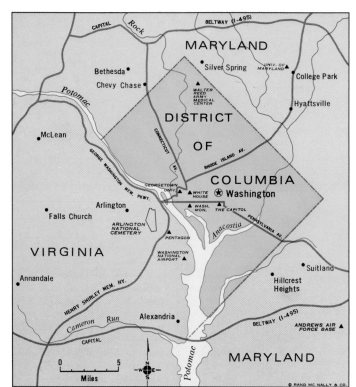

DISTRICT OF COLUMBIA

Area
68 square miles (177 sq. km.)

Population 609,909 people

Principal river Potomac

Highest point 410 feet (125 m.)

Largest city
Washington (587,400 people)

Motto
Justitia omnibus (Justice for all)

Famous people
Alexander Graham Bell, Duke Ellington,
J. Edgar Hoover, John Philip Sousa

The White House, in Washington, D.C., is the home of the president of the United States.

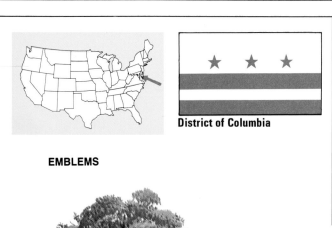

District of Columbia

EMBLEMS

Scarlet Oak

American Beauty Rose

Wood Thrush

Index